The Genteel Poor

The Genteel Poor

a memoir by
William Karl Thomas

MEDIA MAESTRO - BOOK DIVISION

All rights reserved. No part of this book shall be reproduced or transmitted in any form or by any means, electronic, mechanical, magnetic, photographic including photocopying, recording or by any information storage and retrieval system, without prior written permission of the author. No patent liability is assumed with respect to the use of the information contained herein. Although every precaution has been taken in the preparation of this book, the publisher and author assume no responsibility for errors or omissions. Neither is any liability assumed for damages resulting from the use of the information contained herein.

Cover design by William Karl Thomas
Copyright © 2012 by William Karl Thomas

ISBN 978-1-62768-000-4

Printed in the United States of America

This book is a memoir based on the best available information with the attempt to be as accurate and objective as possible. Any errors or omissions are purely accidental and unintentional. Many of the photos were taken by the author, and all other photos were obtained from deceased family members.

Second Edition Published September 2013

❖

MEDIA MAESTRO - BOOK DIVISION
P.O. Box 50672, Tucson AZ 85703
(520) 888-3992
cinemogul@netscape.net
www.mediamaestro.net/books.htm

Dedication

My mother, Katherine, was beautiful, talented, and totally dedicated to her children, even offering to give up her life for them at one point. She survived the pride and vanity of her parental family, and the intrigue and cruelty of her husband's family. Even after her children left home, she embraced the children of her community, integrated the children from the local black school into her library and ultimately the total community, and convinced a small southern town to honor a world famous black sculptor, who happened to have been born and raised there, as the town's most illustrious citizen during their Centennial Celebration. She accomplished all this despite cruelty from her husband, deprivation during the Great Depression, and the challenge of all Southerners to move gracefully into the second half of the Twentieth Century.

This book is dedicated to my mother, Katherine, and to all single mothers who face similar challenges. May you fulfill your parental goals with the courage, resourcefulness, and sustaining love which helped Katherine accomplish hers, and, hopefully, her life, as revealed in these pages, may help inspire you.

To Katherine

Foreword

This is an attempt to provide a social snapshot of a time and place which technology and the wrath of nature may wipe from the face of the earth. I believe I was provided a unique opportunity to observe and come to terms with a transitional period in which humanity abdicates even more of their instinctual talents to opt for cradle-to-grave security and convenience.

Born by the light of a kerosene lamp, I lived to record the life lessons I learned in computer-generated books and electronic media films. I believe there are some lessons that can only be learned from the coincidence of adversity and the talent to observe and evaluate the options those circumstances provide. I fear that future generations may never experience the challenge to recognize and preserve the options I believe in; to survive the immediate, to prioritize the good, and to let go of the bad.

In the time span of this book, four generations of my family survived the Confederate War, World War I, the Great Depression, and World War II, only to narrow down to a dead end branch on our family tree. Just as Hurricane Katrina swept away centuries of architecture and infrastructure from the New Orleans and Gulf Coast regions, so I fear that the loss of so many families from that region, just like the loss of my family through genealogical attrition, will forever erase the lessons learned and values acquired in the unique environment of this early twentieth century New Orleans/Gulf Coast community.

I hope that sociologists and historians will agree that the people and places in this memoir are subjects worthy of study and reflection. I hope the readers of this book will indulge me in my efforts to be honest, and that they will find something of value and relevant to their own lives. To all whose eyes see these words, and particularly to those who hear these words in their minds and hearts, I thank you for letting me live my youth again through your responsive thoughts and feelings.

William Karl Thomas

Content

Chapter	Title	Page
1	The Cottage	1
2.	Tarzan Oaks	21
3.	Katherine	43
4.	Staten Island	61
5.	New Orleans	81
6.	Checkerboard	101
7.	My Early Business Career	121
8.	The War Years	147
9.	My Early Artistic Career	169
10.	My Peers	191
11.	Hurricane	211
12.	My Teachers	237
Other books by William Karl Thomas		266

Chapter One
THE COTTAGE

Alfred was eight-years-old and very sleepy when our grandmother, Lo, woke him in the middle of the night and brought him into my mother's bedroom to view his newborn little brother, me. He remembers me as disgustingly fat, disturbingly loud, and sporting a full head of hair. Doctor Horton was wiping me clean as I had a bowel movement immediately after birth, probably the result of my mother, Katherine, carrying me a full month over term. I was supposed to have been born on December 25th, but, perhaps, the deity thought that date was inappropriate for me and I was born January 25th, 1933.

Alfred remembers the yellow glow of the kerosene lamps on Doctor Horton's white shirt and the wisps of white hair that fell into his wrinkled face that showed as many liver spots as his forearms where he began to roll down his shirt sleeves. Doctor Horton was probably the principal man in our family at that time. I doubt that he ever made a pass at my mother, but, as a good and generous soul, one of those rare old country doctors who'd rather be right than rich, he was perhaps my mother's chief counselor and a crucial necessity in the poverty of our childhood.

Though we saw little of him, we saw him at our greatest moments of crisis. Whether it was in the old model T coupe driving up to our front gate, or in his waiting room on the second story of that ramshackle building on Main Street, whenever we saw him he was a lifesaver. That bare old waiting room in that faded grey building was always filled with people as poor as us, mostly farmers with dressed chickens or ducks or baskets of vegetables to pay Dr. Horton with in lieu of money.

We didn't even have these commodities to barter, but Dr. Horton carried us and saved our lives many a time for over a decade during the depression. He brought me into the world at 2:25 in the morning, although I could never find that information for would-be astrologers until many years later when I finally deciphered Dr. Horton's scribbly handwriting on my birth certificate. That document also specifies that I am white and legitimate, details which I imagine future archaeologists finding irrelevant and humorous.

Alfred Joseph Thomas, whom everyone called A.J., went back to bed and woke the next morning wondering if he had dreamed about the baby or actually had a new little brother in addition to his four-year-old sister, Thelma. 1933 at the height of the depression was not the greatest time for his mother to be a 33-year-old divorcee with three small children. Even if her father had once been wealthy and even if the courts had awarded a total of $25 a month child support from a husband 2000 miles away in Canada, which he never sent, it was still lousy timing to be a single parent.

But there could have been worse places than Bay St. Louis, Mississippi, to raise children. The little coastal town, perched at the mouth of a beautiful bay with a beautiful beach and located sixty miles east of New Orleans, was just close enough to have a few wealthy city folk with summer homes, yet far enough away to be uncrowded and unhurried. Lola Inez Schmidt, my mother's mother, was one of the wealthy city folk, and the cottage I was born and raised in was one of her two summer homes that sat side by side on Second Street a block from the beach.

Lo had been a widow only a few years when her daughter arrived home after an unsuccessful nine year marriage to a handsome, intelligent, talented young Canadian who couldn't grow up. But being a widow only a few years had not kept Lo, in her naivete, from losing what her husband had left her. He died unexpectedly in his mid-fifties leaving a very large estate almost entirely in property and investments which Lo did not know how to manage nor ultimately keep from the grasp of creditors and loan sharks.

When her daughter arrived home with two small children and a bellyful of me, Lo had little to offer her except the two summer cottages; one to live in and the other to rent for an income. That rental income usually amounted to $25 a month for the three summer months of the year, and rarely ever more than that.

But that little green shuttered three bedroom frame cottage that Lo's husband built with his own hands was probably far better than many people enjoyed during the depression. It was shaded by a beautiful large oak tree in the side yard, a date bearing palm tree in the front yard, and a collection of five pecan trees and three fig trees in the back yard. In the Spring and early Summer, these trees were laced together with a lavender canopy of wisteria vine that filtered the sun above and carpeted the ground below with their blooms. The wisteria had originated in an arbor at the front gate, but had grown throughout the grounds with roots as thick as a man's torso in places and some low hanging loops that served as swings for children.

The cottage was poorly insulated, its' walls having no hollow core. The roof leaked in spots, the single layer flooring allowed drafts in places, and the inadequate plumbing terminated in a cesspool that suffered from a water table three feet below ground level and an open wooden grey water drain to the rear of the lot. The doors hung askew, dust filtered from the cracks in the ceiling boards, and the brick fireplaces in the living room and front bedroom were so poorly designed they belched smoke into the rooms.

But it was a home in all the warmest and most positive senses of a home. A place where children could mark a chalk circle on the worn Persian rug and play marbles in the living room on a cold winter's day. The aromas of chicory coffee and brown flour gravy could not be lessened by the modesty and unreliability of the kerosene kitchen stove. The leaky icebox offered little problem as we could rarely afford ice, but when we could it provided the treasure of chilled watermelon and our mother's magic formula for delicious toppings on snowballs made with a hand ice shaver.

And when all the kitchen equipment failed, as often it did, meals, sometimes as modest as popcorn with oleomargarine on it, were cooked in the open living room fireplace. These fires were often fueled by wood scavenged from nearby swamps as the single winter's supply of one cord of pinewood rarely lasted past Christmas.

Added to the aroma of poor man's food and smokey fireplaces was the eternal smell of glue and the thinner used in silver and gold paints on the endless variety of craft projects Katherine used to distract her children from the poverty of their environment. Hunger can make brown flour gravy on a slice of bread taste delicious. Cold can make even the most inefficient fireplace a warm and welcome hearth. The derision, or even crueler pity, of a community can make a mother's love a salvation.

Ironic in the midst of our poverty, were the furnishings in our home. Though our staples were grits and bologna, a menu my brother and sister learned to hate, we ate this poor man's fare on Limoge china with Old Colonial sterling flatware and fine Irish linen on a carved mahogany dining table. The centerpiece was a large pewter apern of Persephone rising from the sea surrounded by cupids and dolphins. Our walls were adorned with Drysdale paintings commissioned by Lo for the exact niches in her home, hand colored stone lithographs and steel etchings by noted artists, and occasional autographed works by friends of the family such as political cartoonist John Churchill Chase. The curved glass fronted china cabinets displayed a dazzling array of curios from my grandfather's world travels and sundry family heirlooms in gold, silver, pewter, opal, amethyst, goldstone, alabaster, onyx, and Lalique glass.

But the glass-fronted bookcases held the greatest treasures for three small children whose place in the real world outside that little cottage was at the bottom of the ladder. Those books from *Nancy Drew* and *Bomba The Jungle Boy* to Shakespeare and Chaucer, those books with their leather and gold leaf bindings and their steelcuts and full color lithographs of the artistic, architectural, and environmental panorama of the world, those books with their words of wisdom and their wings of imagination helped us to understand and endure our plight and appreciate our intellectual and spiritual wealth while our tummies rumbled and our peers derided us.

Also displayed on our walls were family photographs and some of my grandfather's works, his most elaborate, historical, or sentimental copper engravings framed or made into trays or bowls. These would be shown to visitors by holding them in front of a mirror so the design or wording would be legible left to right and the viewer could see the complex illustration for a turn of the century Mardi Gras invitation or read an invitation to a reception for Teddy Roosevelt or my grandparents wedding announcement.

The family photographs did not lay any claims to a celebrated lineage, but gave a sense of continuity and direction to the compounding of knowledge and ability rather than material wealth.

On my father's side, the only claim to fame was in being a cousin of Buffalo Bill Cody. Beyond that, my father would stop searching through his Welch and German ancestry each time he'd run up against a noble coat of arms that was bar sinister.

On my mother's side, her father's parents came from the German side of Switzerland where my great grandfather had invented the first machine to weave ribbons with patterns and edging at high speed, the first sample of which rested in those curved glass fronted china cabinets and in wavy imperfect Gothic German declared 'In God We Trust.' The old man had been decorated by the Swiss Government for his invention, but was disgruntled with Swiss politics and immigrated to New York with his wife and the first two of ten children.

One of the sons, Jake, became a prominent engraver for the Federal Mint. His brother Will, my grandfather William John Schmidt, apprenticed as an engraver in New York, but, when his father beat him for cashing one of his own paychecks to buy a shirt, the boy ran away to Mexico, became a telegrapher, and was well on his way to success by the time he moved to New Orleans.

My great grandmother, Belzora Greene Stanselle, was known to her daughter, Lola, by the pet name "Mimi." She was born and raised in the vicinity of Natchez, Mississippi, probably a descendant of the 'Voyager' gentleman who surveyed and mapped Louisiana, and obviously of Scotch, Irish, and Indian ancestry. She escaped her rural origins by marrying Charles Magee during the Civil War period. Charles Magee was a traveling schoolteacher who provided the only formal education available to the people in those areas and was probably one of the most glamorous images a backwoods girl was likely to see.

Mimi bettered her position in life through successive marriages, but had only the one child, Lola, born in St. Louis, Missouri, during her first marriage. We don't know how many times she married, but most of her last years were spent in those little cottages in Bay St. Louis where she went by her maiden name, Stanselle.

During the critical part of Lo's childhood, Mimi was married to an elderly German shopkeeper known as

Papa App, and Lo adopted his name and a fondness for the old gentleman who taught her to read and write German. Her fluency in German no doubt played a part in Will Schmidt's attraction to her and their love letters in exquisite German penmanship resided in Lo's desk nestled in the bay window of her house on Patton Street in New Orleans. During extended visits there as a small child, I'd often see grey haired round faced Lo, her overfull muumuu bedecked figure barely contained by the classic Greek chair before the desk, reading poetry in German aloud but softly to herself from Will's letters as tears streamed down her cheeks.

Will was a man for all seasons. After his move from Mexico to New Orleans, he chanced to see Lola Inez App and her mother, Mimi, on St. Charles Avenue, and became enamored of her. I'm sure he was aggressive enough to make her acquaintance and I suspect her mother, Mimi, was shrewd enough to perceive and cultivate Will as an opportunity for Lola. Will married Lola and, with his zest for adventure and challenge, began to build his fortune.

Will's talents were many, his business acumen phenomenal, and his personality gregarious and scintillating. With them he built the leading engraving firm in the South, staffed it with some of his brothers, and compounded his fortune with investments and real estate deals that found poor Lola frantically moving into bigger and better houses while Will sold the old ones at ever increasing profits.

Will was the personification of the word indomitable. Fate had never been able to make him doubt that life was a joyous affair and he was capable of anything to which he aspired. He was ambidextrous and would engrave copper plates with both hands simultaneously. He would invent technology as it was needed. He took his mother-in-law's general store in Bay St. Louis, cut it in half and made two summer cottages out of it, then built a third, the one I was raised in, on the corner next to them. He taught himself to play a variety of musical instruments from the harmonica to the guitar, the mandolin, and the piano. He'd join any and every fraternal and professional organization that asked him to, and he became a 33rd degree Mason via the Scottish Rite so he could maintain his friends of Jewish and other faiths. He loved to travel, to sing, to dance, to admire and be admired by the ladies.

He supported philanthropic projects and, when he could find no doctors to volunteer duty in free clinics he proposed funding, he took years away from his business to attend medical school in Tennessee where he became an M.D., only to return to New Orleans and offer his services freely.

Finally, when Will wanted to sell their most recent house on Patton Street a block from Audubon Park, Lola put her foot down and refused to budge, feeling that, with two small girls, it was time to establish some roots and some continuity to their daily life.

Thelma Inez Schmidt was born during the 1890's and Katherine Ida Schmidt, my mother, was born in 1900. Thelma was more introverted and resembled Lola in appearance, while Katherine seemed to favor and be favored by her father. Will probably wanted a son, and Katherine became a tomboy to cater to him. I'm sure Will was too wise and compassionate to let Thelma suffer any disparity in his affection for his daughters, but Katherine was too young and naive to be aware of how blatant her love for her father was or how much her efforts to please him influenced her development.

Both girls were exceptionally talented and given the finest training from an early age. Thelma performed as a child dancer with some of the vaudeville greats of her day, but her conservative mother never allowed her to be paid nor assume professional status and, as Lo felt, the attendant stigma of show business.

Likewise, Katherine was allowed to work at

china painting and jewelry making in the artisan shops centered around her father's engraving firm, but only as a hobby and never for remuneration. The girls were sent to a parochial 'music conservatory' in Tennessee for 'finishing' where Thelma's piano and Katherine's violin studies prompted teachers to beg Lola to let them enter concert careers, but it was still 'show biz' to Lo and the girls despaired as they saw equal and lesser peers go on to successful music careers.

Lo felt the girls should merely prepare themselves for the social marriage market, and even that Lo presided over too closely for the potential suitor's comfort. Thelma was just barely attractive and, though considered beautiful by some, Katherine presented certain challenges what with driving an ambulance for her father into all those sordid ghettos where he maintained free clinics. By the age of 23, Katherine considered herself an old maid, and her older sister, Thelma, after an abortive attempt to become a nun, resigned herself to carving out a career in business in lieu of ever marrying.

Will's gregarious nature compelled him to befriend any and everyone who stood still long enough to have their hand shaken. One such acquaintance was a wiry little Canadian named Ezra Thomas who maintained a wholesale jewelry supply firm in Buffalo, New York, and supplied the artisans around Will's firm during Ezra's annual sales tour of the States. Ezra had welcomed the opportunity to avail himself of Will's hospitality and valuable contacts. Upon his return to his home in Canada, he told his four sons about the wealthy New Orleans engraver and his beautiful but racy daughter, Katherine, who drove cars, wore men's clothes, and beat men at their own game.

His second eldest son, Erle, was within a year of Katherine's age, was still unsettled after his World War I experience of being gassed at the front lines, and found sufficient excuse to pass through New Orleans while making a business trip to acquire tropic specimens for his floral business.

Erle met Katherine at one of the rare moments Lola was traveling with Will and the girls were not under Lo's smothering wing. Erle was disappointed to find a naive and proper girl instead of the fast and free image his conservative father had painted, but was suitably impressed with the girl's beauty and the family's wealth. He proposed marriage, motivated mostly by his father's interest in the Schmidt's wealth and least of all by any understanding or sincere intention of establishing a family. Katherine married him, moved to Canada, bore three children, and spent nine years of hell before admitting to herself, much less her conservative mother, that she had made a dreadful mistake.

A.J. was born in Canada, two months premature, I suspect a result of Erle's abuse of Katherine during her pregnancy which he did not want, but would not take measures to prevent. Erle knew the facts of life, but just barely, and not as much of the mechanics of reproduction as a doctor's daughter. He left the burden of birth control, as well as contending with his ignorance, to a woman who both wanted a family and who he could intimidate and overpower.

A.J. inherited rickets from both his parents, but Erle and his family led Katherine to believe her family was the sole source. A.J. had soft delicate bones, a soft spot in his skull that lasted into adolescence, and fused elbow joints which were surgically separated and reconstructed when he was seven. Katherine enlisted all the medical expertise she could garner when he was born and applied Swedish massage and every therapy she could learn from the time of his birth to post adolescence. As a result of her ministrations, the private tutors she provided with her father's money to compensate for his inability to enter school until the age of nine, and the cultural trappings of his home environment, A.J. became an intellectual, a mystic, and finally a colorful hermit living in the woods. As a result of his father's rejection, his psyche faced unimaginable challenges over which he ultimately triumphed.

Erle forced Katherine to abort her second pregnancy at the hands of an alcoholic doctor who almost killed her, so Katherine fled to New Orleans with her third pregnancy.

Thelma Margaret Thomas, named after Katherine's sister and sister-in-law, was born in 1928 in New Orleans, whole and healthy, wiry and hyper-active, and much like her father's family in looks and nature. She wound her father around her infinitely little finger, innocently compounding Erle's rejection of his firstborn son, and learned the guile of her father's clan which thrived on family and business intrigue. Her boundless drive and energy developed courage to the point of audacity, salesmanship to the point of invincibility, and tenacity to the point of frustration.

Throughout her early life she loved the battle so much more than the victory that she never knew when to lay down her arms or what indeed was the prize she sought. At times she squandered her great beauty, strength, and health on less than noble people and causes, mistaking admiration for love and love for weakness. Like her mother, she would never be conscious of how blatant her love for her father was and how much her efforts to please him would influence her development.

Though this wiry little monkey faced girl would grow up to grace the covers of magazines, live in some of the most beautiful places in the world, and keep the company of celebrities and presidents of nations, she would waste decades being torn between the lies of those who shared her penchant for intrigue and the truths of those who loved her.

Erle aborted Katherine's fourth pregnancy with his own hands, a grisly and ultimate trauma for a woman, now past thirty, who could no longer girlishly accept Lo's admonition to live by her mistakes. After nine years, she finally admitted to herself that her children's very survival, much less her own, lay separate from the man she had married. When shortly thereafter she knew she was pregnant for a fifth time, and before Erle could know anything about it, Katherine left for New Orleans with her children, resigned to divorcing Erle.

    She took nothing of value but her life and those entrusted to her. Her father had died some two years prior and her mother was going through a period of adjustment which threatened the stability of their former wealth. Katherine was seriously ill from Erle's abuse and the two primitive abortions she had endured. When she arrived home, she was advised to terminate her fifth pregnancy as neither she nor the child were likely to survive. She refused.

    She settled into the little cottage at the corner of Second and St. George Streets prepared to die in childbirth, if necessary, and let Lo raise her small son and daughter. It was the height of the depression and many others were suffering similar plights all around.

    This was a family with no adult male, just a naive confused Lola, recently widowed and on the threshold of old age, her seriously ill and pregnant daughter, and her two small grandchildren. Even Thelma Schmidt, the other daughter who had finally embarked on a business career with RCA, was living in far off New York City.

    In lieu of the ready cash which Lo lacked the knack for deriving from her considerable holdings, she furnished the cottage sumptuously with the costly trappings of her former lifestyle. The joy of having a new generation of family restored to her after the loss of her husband, coupled with a tinge of guilt at not being able to adequately provide their more immediate bare necessities, led her to surround Katherine and her children with Lo's most valued and revered mementos.

Though it never occurred to her that some of these valuables might be converted into the food and cash that were so desperately needed, she probably did consider that Katherine should be surrounded by these things if she was indeed to die, and perhaps the message in them about her family and their ideals might influence her survival.

The third cottage had been sold years before, and the remaining two had never been wired for electricity. Cylindrical white candles an inch in diameter and six inches long came in boxes of twelve and sold for a penny a piece, a price which escalated annually. In a silver or brass candlestick holder, with its' round teacup-like handle, they were more durable and safer in the hands of children than the kerosene lamps. Besides, you could cut a candle to a prescribed length and it would automatically go out after a child fell asleep.

Kerosene lamps were the principle illumination with their tall glass 'hurricane' chimneys and elaborately patterned pressed glass bases where one could see the remaining supply of amber fuel we called 'coal oil.' These lamps flavored the nights with their distinctive aroma and golden light.

There was an indoor bathroom, but no water heater. Water was heated in pots on the kitchen kerosene stove or in the fireplace and poured into the tub until an equilibrium of volume and temperature was reached, a losing proposition on a cold winter's day. The heavy old claw-footed cast iron tub could suck the heat out of five pots of boiling water before it lost its' own icy chill, although, once heated, it would retain its' warmth long enough for you to fall asleep in the tub, waking with chattering teeth and wrinkled skin.

But it was early summer when Katherine moved in and there was time to put down some kitchen and bathroom linoleum, even if it would soon be creased by the cracks in the floorboards, it would still serve as protection against the elements.

Kitchen counter and bathroom walls were further protected by floral printed oilcloth that would peel and droop and require annual replacement. Katherine had a penchant for floral prints and, during the art nouveau period, for the combination of pink and ivory. Her bedroom was always a sea of pink and ivory and flowers and satin.

Katherine was periodically bedridden due to 'female problems.' Being an intermittent invalid and desperately poor kept her from going out except on rare occasions. But her dressing table was an integral prop for her ego rather than her vanity.

Erle's cruelty had been mental as well as physical and he had been the only person in her life to cast doubts on her beauty or ability. But for his cruelty, she would have been at her best at all times, and at her best she was a classic beauty blessed with a rare brain and heart and the courage to use them. But his abuse had tarnished that beauty and taxed that courage.

Katherine's dressing table was a classic 1930's Hollywood version of milady's boudoir, only in Technicolor. She mimicked the hairstyles of Claudette Colbert and Jean Harlow, and rivaled their beauty. The quality of the elaborately contoured beveled mirror, the cut crystal perfume bottles with carved jade stoppers, the personally engraved sterling toiletry set, the carved ivory and genuine tortoise shell combs, and the vast array of jewelry, a substantial part of which was precious and valuable, these details far surpassed any collection of props with which Hollywood ever dressed a set.

Yet, like Hollywood, if the camera backed away from this beautiful woman in her pink satin dressing gown staring questioningly at her reflection in an elaborate mirror surrounded by beautiful accessories, one would eventually see the limits of the fantasy which was a small island in a larger more modest, if not squalid, environment.

Doctor Horton was not one to cater to beautiful daughters of rich men. As a country doctor he had played God for almost fifty years to untold numbers of people. Medicine was just a means of salvaging souls, and egos, neither his nor theirs, had nothing to do with it. It mattered not that Katherine was the daughter of Dr. William J. Schmidt, a greatly revered fellow colleague, a philanthropist, a 33rd degree Mason, a veritable saint among men. Katherine was just another pregnant girl in the midst of a horrendous national depression, not a very wise girl to have accepted so much abuse for so long, and perhaps a trifle vain, though only a doctor who had seen the inner sanctum of milady's boudoir might have reason to suspect.

The thin line of Dr. Horton's unsmiling mouth tightened as his flinty eyes flashed from under bushy white eyebrows at the girl who defied his advice to abort a potentially lethal pregnancy. He had no time for maternal melodramatics. But he watched with growing respect her dedication to her children, her therapy for the impaired firstborn son, and her courage in coping with their circumstances and her approaching delivery.

He advised her to trust her bodily instincts and eat whatever she felt like. She was concerned about rickets, with due cause as it was inherent in both sides of the family, and tried to concentrate on calcium products. For better or worse, she developed a passion for sweetened condensed milk, which doubtless contributed to the fact that I weighed slightly over twelve pounds at birth. I sometimes wonder if she acquired such a taste from Lo who had an insatiable sweet tooth and eventually became a diabetic.

Doctor Horton's model T coupe arrived and departed frequently from the front gate covered by the blossoming wisteria arbor. The palm tree in the front yard gave up its' dates to children, the fig trees in the back yard gave up their overripe fruit to noisy bluejays, and the wisteria canopy above and carpet below gave up its' lavender bloom to the torrential rains at summer's end. The pecan trees shed their leaves, the thorn trees turned brown, and only the great oak tree that shaded the little cottage held fast its evergreen hue against the coming winter.

The winter's on the Gulf Coast were bitingly cold. Though it rarely snowed or hailed, and that never stayed on the ground for long, the humidity was always in the nineties and when the temperature was freezing you might as well have been encased in a block of ice. All the windows had exterior louvered shutters, a necessary protection during summer hurricanes, but they were in disrepair and the howl of the wind played its own counterpoint rattling the shutters and whistling through the cracks in the walls.

My debut was scheduled for Christmas and, at that time, Lo attached the shiny colored metal candle holders to the Christmas tree. They were in decorative shapes and attached like clothes pins to the limbs of the tree, each holding a large birth day cake size candle. She arranged the beautiful ivory colored figurines in a manger scene beneath the tree. She made sure there were gifts and treats for everyone. On the mantlepiece she lit candles for each departed family member or friend. She lit one for her mother 'Aunt' Mimi, her stepfather 'Papa' App, her husband 'Daddy' Bill, and she wondered with heavy heart if the following year she'd be lighting one for her daughter Katherine.

Christmas came and Christmas went and I had not arrived. The more Doctor Horton diagnosed Katherine's complications, the more Lo realized what Katherine had suffered in Canada. She knew Katherine had suffered silently rather than concern her ailing father, then her widowed mother, and she knew Katherine had persevered in part because of Lo's conservative attitudes about marriage and divorce.

Lo was religious in a passive sort of way. She

had evolved through various Christian sects, including her husband's Lutheran background, through Catholicism until, during my youth, she arrived happily at the Rosicrucian faith. I know not by what manner or faith she practiced her religion in the winter of '32 and '33, but I have no doubt she prayed a lot and even repented a little.

Doctor Horton faced the agony of a caring practitioner of that day in a little town where there was no hospital to perform a cesarian in when it was needed. He had no choice but to keep a watchful eye in a stony impassive face so the two women could not see his serious doubts. He often masked his deep concern by being dictatorial and irascible, but, in the last few days when I kept him in constant attendance on Katherine, they knew he was as worried and fearful as they were.

We are the product of so many different elements, things that transpire from before our conception and throughout our life. From the midpoint of prenatal development, everything that impinges on our senses is recorded in the computer we carry around within us. I thank my mother for that extra month in her womb which I'm convinced helped me find the buttons on my computer so early in life. I am blessed with the opportunity to know from whence I came, the desire to understand it, and, I hope, the ability to appreciate its' best and its' worst.

Perhaps I was reluctant to meet this world. Perhaps I needed to be overly prepared to meet this world. But meet this world I did, and not with a whimper, but with a night shattering yell. I greeted Katherine, I greeted Lo, I greeted Doctor Horton and my sleepy brother and sister. They and all the neighbors knew, Katherine's fifth and final child was not stillborn. He was fat, he was sassy, and he wasn't still from January 25th, 1933, through the rest of his life.

This Page: House at 6313 Patton Street, *(left to right)*: Katherine, the Nanny, Thelma, Mimi, Lola, Will, the Housekeeper, Aunt Mary, and the Gardener.

Left Page: *(top left)* Mimi Belzora Greene Stanselle; *(top right)* Mr. & Mrs. Schmidt; *(center left)* Lola Schmidt; *(center right)* Dr. William Joseph Schmidt; *(bottom of 'V')* Thelma & Katherine Schmidt; Bottom *(left to right)* Alfred Joseph Thomas, Thelma Margaret Thomas, the author, and Katherine Schmidt Thomas, circa 1937.

Chapter Two
TARZAN OAKS

One block from our little cottage was a beautiful beach with sand as white and as fine as confectioner's sugar, and on that beach was a particular oak tree, a gigantic old moss covered tree we called Tarzan Oaks because its limbs swept low enough to touch the ground in some places, and even the smallest child could climb into it and experience the world of Tarzan and Jane. We are tree people, the people of that area in general and my family in particular.

We don't presume to know which came first, a spirit or a thing, but we do know that all things have spirits. Perhaps my family inherits this knowledge from the tiny drop of Indian blood we possess, or perhaps we deduced it through intelligence, observation, and logic. But we do believe it. The natural and man made curios in the curved china closet, the tool we pick up in our hand; metal, rock, and living fibre in all its colors and textures, all these we know can bear witness, remember, and respond to good and evil. We talk to these things, and, whether they respond or are simply mirrors we invest with our own reflections, we learn so much from our dialogue with them.

Many a time I lay in the curve of Tarzan Oak's branches, the bark scratching my back, the sun twinkling through the moss, and the warm salty waves of the bay lapping gently near my toes. This tree was a being who stood taller than any building in our town, had lived longer than any human I shall ever meet, and had witnessed hurricanes and Indian ceremonies and the coming of the new world.

It might have seen the ship of the Portuguese

Gaspar Cortereal who tried to follow Columbus' course a few years after him and in 1502 showed, on the map of his discoveries, the first record of the Florida peninsula and the Gulf Coast to the west.

Perhaps it shaded the Spanish survivors of the 1528 Narvaez expedition who, being defeated by the Indians after they landed at Appalachee Bay to the East, had forged their iron weapons of plunder into hatchets and nails and stitched their shirts into sails for five small handmade escape boats. They traveled from Florida to the mouth of the Mississippi where Narvaez drowned with many of his men in the river's turbulent waters. Only four of the original four hundred men in the Narvaez party survived the tortuous overland trek through Texas and Mexico to find salvation in a Spanish colony.

This tree might have seen Robert Cavalier de LaSalle in 1682 when he explored the area around the mouth of the Mississippi River, or his friend Tonti in 1688 who searched for him in vain.

We know it provided shade for the Choctaw Indians whose village, Chicapoula, was the original town site and who opened many an oyster and dropped many an arrowhead for us to find centuries later beneath Tarzan Oak's branches. What did those Choctaws think, and what did the oak tree think, when they saw the French brothers and explorers Iberville and Bienville land, perhaps on that very spot, on August 25, 1699?

We know what the French thought, because Pericault, the journalist of Bienville's frigate, Le Marin, wrote, "We shortly afterward found a beautiful bay about one league in width, by four in circumference, which was named Bay of St. Louis, because it was on the day of St. Louis that we arrived there. We hunted for three days, and killed 50 deer. Next day we camped at the entrance of bay St. Louis near a fountain of water that flows down from the hills which Moyne Bienville named Belle Fontaine. We hunted several days around this Bay and filled our boats with venison, buffalo, and other game." In December of 1699, Iberville placed a few families, a sergeant, and fifteen men in Bay St. Louis. Bienville went on to found Mobile in 1702 and New Orleans in 1718.

Then, on January 3, 1721, two French ships, La Gironde and La Volage, arrived with 300 persons to settle sites on the Yazoo River, Pascagoula Bay, and Bay St. Louis. A Madame Mezieres was given 17,084 acres in Bay St. Louis for her colonists, and it was never the same for the Choctaws and Tarzan Oaks since.

The oak tree probably wasn't aware when the flags were changed from French to English in 1763, to Spanish in 1793, and back to French in 1800. Ultimately, they spent twenty days in 1803 playing musical flags during which it went from Spain to France to the United States.

The Choctaws, I'm sure, were aware of the changing of flags. If there were any agreements made with the Choctaws, I'm sure each change of flags provided a convenient excuse to annul any obligations to them under the former ruler. The Choctaw in this area were a short, almost yellow skinned, oriental looking people. 233 years after the French landed, there was little evidence of the Choctaw for me to witness.

Among my school peers there were two families that were noticeably Choctaw. One family lived a block away and the older boy used to bully me a lot until I passed him up so many grades in school our paths no longer crossed. He and his sister had a sort of Cro Magnon look, but his younger brother was slighter in build with more delicate Oriental-like features which, despite the incongruity of his blonde hair, was probably more representative of the Choctaw. The other family had two daughters my school age, the older one a raving beauty with brown hair, the younger brunette quite petite and exotic looking, her beauty flawed only by a slight cast in one eye.

These were the only Choctaws I knew, and they were Indian only in their physiogamy. Culturally they were like the other children, many of whom were part Choctaw, but, with the mixture of French and Spanish and Sicilian and Anglo-Saxon, were not discernible.

Of course, two blocks away there was the 'Squaw Man,' an elderly white man with two Choctaw Indian wives. Rumors abounded about the family. It was said the women were sisters, that he had purchased them as slaves, and that he had syphilis. The only thing I knew for sure was that he had gout and could be seen seated on the front porch of his little house which sagged in the middle, his swollen foot on a pillow and the two Indian ladies silently attending him while he fumed and grouched and spit tobacco into the un-kept front yard. But walking home late at night past the little house with a kerosene lamp glow coming through the curtained window was enough to feed many a fantasy about the only man in town with two wives, at least two concurrent wives.

I'm sure the oak tree observed the passing of the Choctaw with regret. Their children had climbed its limbs with bare feet, their women had fed its roots with nature's excess, and their wise men had talked to it with reverence and respect.

The new Europeans, who couldn't decide which flag they would fly or language they would speak, who came because of the beauty they saw with their eyes but were blind to the damage they did with their hands, whose children climbed the tree with hobnail boots and carved hieroglyphs in its bleeding bark, they did not talk to the tree as did the Choctaw.

Within sight of the tree in the Gulf outside the mouth of the bay was Cat Island, so called because it was shaped like a sleeping cat, although rumor has it that it once abounded with cat-like animals. During the War of 1812, the British fleet was seeking the mouth of the Mississippi River to invade New Orleans before

General Jackson could arrive at its defense. The British sighted a hunting party on Cat Island led by Spanish Grandee Don Juan Cuevas, Official Emissary from the Court of Spain and an avid hunter and fisherman, probably bent on hunting the cat-like creatures on the island.

The British landed and tried to force information regarding the water route to New Orleans from the Grandee whose honor insured his silence and loyalty to his American hosts. While the Grandee and his party floundered in chains aboard the British flagship, the British navy floundered among the countless inlets and bayous that masked the true entrance to the great river, and General Jackson arrived to fortify New Orleans and win an historic victory over the tardy British, a victory that decided whether this vast area would be English or American for centuries to come.

For his valor and fidelity, Don Juan Cuevas was gifted with Cat Island tax free for all time. He returned from Spain with his new bride to build a mansion in Bay St. Louis, not far from Tarzan Oaks, and founded one of the largest families in the area, many of whose children climbed the great oak tree.

The mixture of Spanish and French families produced an ethnic group known as Creole, a blend of genes, language, architecture, cuisine, and other cultural attributes which were distinct to Southern Louisiana and Mississippi. Creoles were also the earliest European rulers in Haiti and a rare few other West Indian cities where French and Spanish aristocracy intermarried. After the slave revolution in Haiti and the Civil War in America, many fair-skinned ex-slaves of Creole extraction referred to themselves as Creole until, today, unknowledgeable persons assume Creole is a mixture of French, Spanish, and Negro. This false assumption is sometimes considered offensive by 'pure' Creoles of today who resent hearing their friend from California announce that his black housekeeper is also 'Creole.'

Another mixture distinct to this area is the 'Cajun,' a mixture of Indian, usually Choctaw, and the Acadian French who were driven out of Acadia, Canada, by the English in 1755 and migrated to New Orleans and the Gulf Coast in large numbers thereafter. Cajuns speak a French 'patois' which is comprehensible only to them, though much of its vocabulary and idiomatic expression have become everyday language in the south, as well as their cuisine which was in part immortalized in the pop song *Jambalaya, Crawfish Pie, File Gumbo.*

Originally they inhabited the swamps and bayous which no one else could tolerate or navigate, and which shielded them from the series of wars and territorial conflicts. They would sometimes emerge to fight the cause of the French and ultimately the United States, but, in between, they would allow their hidden retreats to become havens for pirates and sometimes man their ships.

When I was growing up, about half the French named families in town were proud to be known as Cajun. They were farmers, fishermen, schoolteachers, and shopkeepers. The other half of the French named families usually traced their lineage directly to France and some as high as Napoleon's private circle.

Another distinctly American breed that came to the Gulf Coast sometime during this period was that of Black Americans. The forebears of Black Americans first came to this continent in 1619 as African slaves arriving on a Dutch ship on the Eastern seaboard. By 1790, four years after the American Revolution, blacks comprised twenty percent of the American population.

Their 'migration' to the Gulf Coastal areas was not a voluntary one and commenced more than a century after their introduction to the Northeast when, in the mid 1700's, cane sugar began massive cultivation in New Orleans. The first American sugar refinery was built in New York City in 1689, but the raw product was imported from the West Indies long before it became a principal crop in the deep South. Sugar initiated the agrarian empire in the deep South which was expanded with the invention of the cotton gin in 1793 and the technology for cultivating rice during the next century. The black labor force expanded proportionately to become the dominant percentage of the population in most agrarian areas of the South.

But this was not true of the immediate coastline where the land was swampish, brackish with salt water, and prone to hurricanes which did not favor such crops. Bay St. Louis had a minimal black population, mostly employed as domestics and mercantile labor, and a greater number of Freedmen than most other areas supported. The cultural, intellectual, and social mix of the town created an overwhelming majority of 'closet abolitionists' who openly denounced the abuses of slavery and coolly tolerated the law of the land on the subject.

A Catholic church was built in 1848, a boy's school four years later by its pastor, and a girl's school a year later by three Sisters from Havre, France. Thirteen years later, in 1868, the succeeding church pastor built St. Rose deLima, a Negro parochial school which was maintained when I was growing up by the Blue Sisters, a European teaching order. Little wonder that Bay St. Louis became the home of the first of the only two Negro seminaries in America, which was integrated in my childhood decades before the civil rights movement.

The town also honored Richmond Barthe, a world famous black sculptor born and raised in Bay St. Louis, as its most outstanding citizen of the century during its Centennial Celebration.

Anglo-Saxon names began to appear in Bay St. Louis most noticeably when, in 1790, the Spanish Government made a land grant to Thomas Shields in his name, including the shoreline area of Bay St. Louis which was renamed Shieldsborough, a name it sustained until shortly after the Civil War. The War of 1812 brought an end to international conflict over the area and provided a peaceful era for the town to develop as a resort for wealthy Natchez planters and New Orleans families.

A quarter mile from the oak tree a grand hotel was built and, in 1842, owners Edward Milford and Angusters McDonald touted it for "its fine and abundant shade, its excellent drives, a retired resort on the grounds for children and nurses to amuse and recreate themselves, the coolness of the water, the superiority of bathing and washing arrangements."

To this the editor of the New Orleans Daily Picayune added, "Fishing and fine bathing, good eating and drinking, music and dancing, bowling and pistol shooting, billiards, et cetera, contribute some of the amusements and enjoyments at the Bay St. Louis Hotel. But these things are not the only attraction at Milfords. There are lots of beautiful and interesting ladies, who complete the galaxy of splendid attractions now at this desirable resort. Indeed Bay St. Louis is a right pleasant place."

Possibly the hotel served as a brothel, among other things, but I suspect the editor was just trying to pay some personal compliments or was laying it on a little thick to repay the free hospitality he had enjoyed. In any case, I'm sure the oak tree, with its proximity to the hotel, witnessed many a romantic assignation beneath its branches.

But during the Civil War the oak tree saw a sadder picture, the Union Fleet standing offshore affecting the blockade that starved the Confederate Army out of existence. At first it was an occasional Union soldier sneaking ashore at night to steal a chicken or pig in their hunger for fresh foodstuffs. Then there was offshore bombardment, often by sadly misinformed conscripted crews who thought they were entering the mouth of the Mississippi River or approaching some important target.

This area had contributed three famous fighting units to the Confederacy; the Hancock Rebels known in history as Company C, a company of crack shots called the Shieldsborough Rifles, and a cavalry company named the Shieldsborough Dragons. There was a Confederate Army Camp in Shieldsborough named Camp Goode, and it was to this camp the first of my forebears came as a Confederate soldier, but not as a settler.

My maternal great grandfather, Mimi's first husband Charles Magee the traveling schoolteacher, had a brother named John Kinnison Magee. John was the Confederate soldier who was the first of our family known to visit Shieldsborough. Charles and John's mother was a Kinnison, and her parents immigrated from unknown parts of Europe shortly after the Mississippi Valley came under United States jurisdiction. They acquired a sizable tract of acreage 25 miles outside of Natchez in an area known as Hamburg.

When I was quite young we visited the 400 acres still remaining in our family possession, largely through the efforts of my Aunt Thelma whose financial success in New York enabled her to salvage this much from the land grabbers who had been fleecing Lola, her mother.

The original log cabin, which was sizable and still stood when I was a child, was in fair condition. There were the remains of a cotton gin outside the cabin, but someone had been using the gin as a smokehouse for meats and it was damaged beyond repair. The mantlepiece of the stone fireplace inside the cabin was a huge split log, and on its center was a human skull, whose we'll never know. In the attic of the cabin were three 'turkey rifles;' one a double barreled percussion cap, the second a single barreled flintlock with a 'three-finger' load still in its barrel, and the third a flintlock with an unusual single barrel made by winding wire around a form and beating it into an octagonal shape. There were also some powder horns and an old tin box full of papers.

The papers from that tin box were fascinating documents which have since been dispersed to museums. Among them were bills of sale for acreage at 10 cents to 50 cents an acre or bartered for a modest number and variety of farm animals, marriage agreements involving dowries and land commitments, and American paper currency in denominations of less than one dollar.

There was *The White House Cookbook*, printed in 1858, with sections on making medicines, cosmetics, and booze. One recipe for liqueur puzzled me for years with its instruction to put the ingredients in a barrel and "bung it up until Spring." I could never figure out how long it should remain 'bunged up,' until a farmer suggested that, in the time and the climate the book was printed, the ingredients were only harvested and edible for a brief period in the fall, whereas today in southern climates the ingredients are harvested year round.

Also in the tin box was a letter in a beautiful Spenserian handwriting from John Kinnison Magee who, at the age of 22, was stationed as a Confederate soldier at Camp Goode in Shieldsborough where he wrote this, his last letter home, to his father.

Camp Goode, Shieldsborough, Mississippi,
November 23, 1861.
To William K. Magee, esquire
Dear Father,

I embrace the opportunity to answer your letter that I received by Lieutenant Brown. I was well at the time I received your letter and well yet with the exception of my left knee which, unfortunately for me, is sprained, or something else is the matter with it. I am unable to tell the cause, but one thing I know and that is I have to go on my tiptoes and the tendons of my leg are swollen below the knee and above the knee too. They are drawn until it is an impossibility for me to keep my leg in any other shape but the shape of a dog's hind leg ... .There are several here who are always saying that I am working to get a discharge from the Company and I can stand as much fun as anyone in the world, but when they rub it on too thick I can not stand it, and I am the one that wont.

I have no news to write you of any importance, only we are paid off at last, and that was beyond my expectations, for I was content with my lot and could not be convinced of the certainty of our pay until Captain S.E. Rumbel, the Pay Master, brought the needful across the waters of the briny deep. We received $37.46 per head on the 16th of the present month. We got $25 for clothing and $12.46 for our months wages. We only get $11.00 for one month, but we had served more than a month in Confederate Service and, as a matter of course, we received more than the $11.00 for our service.

I am going to give you some of my money for your kindness in sending me the money you sent by Brown. Money in camp was scarce as hen's teeth before we were paid off. I believe that Ransom Hall had $7.50 and I had $7.25 and Marion had $.75, and Marion had loaned Thomas Pickett $2.50. The reason I wrote to you for the money was I did not think we would ever get any from the Confederacy. I didn't need the money, but I thought in time I'd need it.

I am going to try to get a furlough to come home and then I will give you a general description of the Battle Field at Shieldsborough and Pass Christian. I will state that we heard a report yesterday that there were forty men of war at Ship Island. I heard this morning that the report was false. The steamer 'Arrow' just came from Mississippi City and says that there are but four vessels there and they are for the purpose of blockading our ports. I heard this evening that the 3rd Regiment was ordered to the City of New Orleans. This report may be false for we never hear the same thing twice, and a camp is the place for all the lies to originate. I heard that we would have a 'fight' here before three days, but I never thought we would have anything like a fight here unless you would call fighting 'Skeeters' a fight. There are one million and nine to every tent and they can bite harder than any of their size I ever saw. It is the fact if one bites me the bitten place will swell up and look like a yellow jacket had stung it.

While I continue to give you the news of the Camp and other war news, I will inform you that the Oregon and one of the Confederate vessels had a brush with one of Lincoln's vessels. She was shot at three times, but not hurt. The Florida, one of our best gun boats, had a round with the blockade. Lincoln's vessel shot twenty-four bombs at her but missed with every one. She gave the Lincoln fourteen shots and hit Uncle Abe's vessel with three balls which caused Father Abraham to 'About Face' and lumber to safer quarters.

There are seven war vessels anchored in the Lake in sight of us, but they belong to C.S.A. The Arrow is a beautiful small boat and not a Gun Boat, but noted for its swiftness. Its business is to spy. The Oregon has four cannons on it and I can crawl into the mouth of one of them. The Creole (Mail Packet) has one large gun. They are all well prepared for shooting. I think our commerce will end between New Orleans and the Bay of St. Louis before long for the old 'Massachusetts' has been lying off the Island of Cat for some time and I think she will crowd our boats and capture them and then we will have to remove about 25 miles to Pearl River. They can cut off our supplies at any time. The Massachusetts has been in sight of this place and Pass Christian for two months, so I reckon she will not injure us at this late date. I think our seven vessels could give her some shot and shells before she would do all.

Now, before I forget it, I will tell you that Captain Proby sends you his best respects. Lieutenant Perter ditto and Lieutenant Brown also. The Lieutenant

Brown says I can beat Wiley Wharton for circuit clerk next time we run. I am in for trying some county office. I know, and know well, that I am competent to fill any office in the county, and I am for one. I would not run for judge of the circuit nor probate court because I would be acting foolish to do so, but I am in for some office that requires a ready penman, a good speller, and a good officer generally. If anyone is detached from the company to write for the staff officers, I am the one. I wrote for Rumble when he was paying off the companies and there I immortalized my name. S. E. Rumble said, (not in my presence either) that I had the best use of pen of anyone he saw. W. L. Roberts offered to stake all that he was worth that I could write faster and better than any other man in the regiment. I can look at this and think we have some poor scribes here, but I can do better than this.

At this point the faded yellow letter, with its underlining, quotations marks, and excessive capitalization for emphasis, crumbles into illegibility. We do know that John's premonition of a "fight" was correct, even if his sense of false security regarding the passive nature of the Massachusetts lying offshore was not. John Kinnison Magee, born November 29, 1839, lived to see his 23rd birthday, but died in combat April 7, 1862, less than five months after writing his last letter home.

Perhaps he wrote that letter while sitting under Tarzan Oaks. Perhaps he knelt beneath the tree with his compatriots, arms ready, as Union landing boats crossed the Bay to the gleaming sandy shores. We do not know exactly where John Kinnison Magee died, but we do know that the roots of Tarzan Oaks have been irrigated by the blood and tears of many men of many colors and many causes.

Bay St. Louis grew at a snail's pace. There was no local industry other than as a summer resort. The only natural resources were crops harvested somewhat inland and, of course, seafood. Within sight of Tarzan Oaks there was an oyster factory which was originally built on piers out over the water. It was an unsightly tin building and, as early as I can remember in my childhood, it had accumulated enough oyster shells to create a small peninsula totally engulfing the original pilings and providing a driveway from the beach road and a small harbor for the small fleet of shrimp and oyster boats. Before I entered highschool, the oyster factory became defunct, the shrimp and oyster boat fleet moved to Pass Christian, and the unsightly tin building was finally erased by a wrathful mother nature who, in her good taste, always managed to leave Tarzan Oaks standing after each hurricane.

The seafood industry, however, lured another ethnic group into the melting pot of the bay. While America was struggling with its Civil War, southern Europe was ablaze with its own civil wars, particularly Italy. Starting after the American Civil War and continuing over the turn of the century and through World War I, immigration from Italy and Southern Europe escalated from half a million annually to almost five million.

The earliest Italian immigrants came through the port of New York and were largely those foresighted enough to see the impending wars in their country and affluent enough to escape them while also expanding their children's education and their international business interests. They came from the wealthy metropolitan areas in Northern Italy such as Rome, Venice, and Florence, and they settled in New York, Chicago, and the surrounding areas that offered the greatest opportunities as importers and restaurateurs, and the greatest cultural interests in opera and the fine arts.

The successive wars in Italy, however, worked the greatest hardship on the poorer people of Southern

Italy and the ultimate persecution of the vanquished led many to seek survival, as much as opportunity, in the United States. For decades after the major wars in Italy, the political ripples of their aftermath sent waves of Southern Italians to American shores, just as the aftermath of the war between the states sent many impoverished southerners to work in northern factories rather than face a reconstruction era in which a member of any family who had a family member who served the Confederacy could neither vote nor hold office.

A goodly portion of immigrants from Southern Italy were Neapolitans and Sicilians and were looked down upon by the relatively affluent established Italian-Americans because they were poor, swarthy, and, at the time of their arrival, were members of a defeated unpopular political faction. Their poverty and ostracization led large numbers arriving in the North to be restricted to ghettos and exploited, and this motivated them to migrate further. Many were fishermen from the warm Mediterranean and were drawn to the similar environment of the Gulf Coast.

Added to this was the rise of New Orleans to the status of being the nation's second largest seaport, plus an immense coastline whose many bays and inlets had long sheltered pirates and smugglers seeking an easy unguarded portal to the New World. Perhaps more than one unregistered unannounced European ship unloaded its hapless human cargo beneath the moonlit limbs of Tarzan Oaks.

In any case, Bay St. Louis, like New Orleans, had added to its cultural stew a healthy portion of Italian names, talents, and cuisine. Since that period, there has been little influx of new ethnic seasoning to the pot. Perhaps a few displaced persons from World War II, or Cuban or Vietnamese refugees, but they mostly came after my youth in the Bay.

Let me review the recipe of this ethnic potpourri, the chronology of the peoples who have landed, loved, picnicked, and prayed beneath the shade of Tarzan Oaks. The first we know of were the Choctaws. There is a strong possibility the Spanish were the first Europeans there around 1502 (Cortereal, Narvaez, La Salle, Tonti). There is definite record that the French were there in 1699 (Iberville and Bienville) and were the first permanent European settlers no later than 1721 (Madame Mezieres). In the latter half of the 1700's, Creoles shared the sandy beaches with Cajuns, Black Americans, and Anglo Saxons. A century later, Italians added the final spice to the mix.

    The sounds of many dialects and the aroma of many dishes wafted through the limbs of the great oak tree, and it looked down tolerantly, benevolently, and equally upon them all.

    Among these diverse humans who tread upon its roots, Tarzan Oaks looked down upon a latecomer, my great grand mother, Mimi, who was the first of our family I know of to settle in Bay St. Louis around the turn into the 20th century. I don't know exactly when, but I remember hearing that when her son-in-law, Will Schmidt, built the summer cottage next to her little store, he was stymied by the shortage of building materials during World War I, and the shortcuts and compromises he made in its construction led to the drafty nights and smoky fireplaces we complained about as children.

    After leaving her girlhood in Hamburg, Mississippi, Mimi had traveled with her first husband, Charles Magee the traveling schoolteacher, through such places as Knoxville, Chattanooga, and Memphis, Tennessee, where photos taken indicate there were relatives to visit, if not residences resided in for any length of time. It is definite they resided in St. Louis, Missouri, certainly long enough for Mimi's only daughter, Lola, to be born in 1876, and possibly long enough for Charles Magee to expire. Mimi probably learned the mercantile business from Papa App, who was probably her second husband and who, according to another 19th century photo, operated a shoe store in St. Louis, Missouri. Lola was very fond of Papa App and assumed his name when he adopted her.

We do not know all that transpired between that period and the later years when Mimi settled in the Bay. One photo bears the maker's rubber stamp reading, "Mrs. B. G. APP, Successor to C. F. Clark, McComb, Miss," which seems to indicate she (Belzora Greene App) operated a photo studio purchased from C. F. Clark in McComb, Mississippi, at some point after Papa App died and before she moved to New Orleans.

We do know, from turn of the century photos, that Mimi's little store on Second Street in Bay St. Louis sported the latest in ladies finery in its two bay windows, and had large signs declaring, "All Feeds 1 Cent."

Mimi was a strong and independent woman. She provided for herself with a cow, a plow mule, chickens, and a sizable kitchen garden in the backyard at Bay St. Louis, which included a great variety of herbs. No doubt some of those herbs were used in her practice of witchcraft, and she taught Lola some of her occult practices as learned from the sixth and seventh books of Moses.

I remember the time we children prevailed upon Lo to defend our little Bay cottage from the unwelcome visits of an obnoxious elderly neighbor lady who was forever borrowing from our meager larder and nauseating the smallest children with sloppy kisses. Lo self consciously burned some ingredients in an incense burner and recited an incantation that sounded like snatches of Greek and Latin, and when the old lady visited later that day she almost tripped on the front steps, seemed so shaken she faltered in her vain efforts to borrow food from us, and never returned to our house again.

Most whites did not know of or place credence

in Mimi's talents as a witch, but most blacks were quite convinced and accorded her a healthy respect if not a fearful wide berth.

There was a huge bullfrog that lived under the front porch of the cottage and would come out and sit on the arm of Mimi's porch rocker when she would rock there in the twilight and early evening. Many considered the pet bullfrog to be Mimi's witch's 'familiar.'

But Mimi was also a Christian and a good soul whose hardiness and indomitable spirit had helped her survive most of her relatives and in-laws. An alcoholic brother, Wilson Stanselle, lived for a while in Mimi's home. For a few years Uncle Billy, who had been a Union soldier and married one of the Kinnison girls after the Confederate War, lived there and carved from a tree in the backyard the intricate novelties, wooden chains with segments of balls trapped in a wooden cage and tiny compartments with sliding panels, which rested among the family mementos in the china cabinet. Beside Uncle Billy's carvings were Uncle Jayford's Confederate Uniform buttons. Because Jayford Kinnison had been a Confederate soldier, his widow, Aunt Mary, was allowed to spend her remaining years at Beauvoir, Confederate President Jefferson Davis' beach home eighteen miles from the Bay which, when I was growing up, was still maintained as an 'old folks home' for Confederate veterans and their widows.

In Mimi's last years, probably her only remaining family available to her were her visits to Aunt Mary at Beauvoir and her contact with her daughter, Lola. In Mimi's last letter to Lo, before Mimi died in 1930, she spoke of her little cottage in the Bay. She wrote:

My Precious One,
   Your dear sweet letter to hand. Darling, you will never know how much I appreciate it. I wish I was with you so you could tell it all for I know it was a good

omen.

The ice was all over the oak tree. Ice everywhere so I like to froze, but thank our dear Lord I had good bed, good fire to sit by.

Got a nice letter from Aunt Mary and a few lines from Thelma, also Kay. No news. Things are not quite so wet as they were. Nice and warm today. Makes one feel like going to the woods.

Yes, dear heart, we will have a home yet. This is the first real home I ever had since my childhood days, but it took something just to think the cause, but I will buck up and carry on for things will come right yet.

How is your tenant coming on? Do write, if only a line. I do love you both. Keep well. Darling, watch out for the autos, they don't care who they run over.
Lovingly,
Mimi

Lola was to lose her mother and her husband within a year of each other. These losses would probably influence Katherine's reluctance to admit to her family that her marriage was failing.

Perhaps, in sorting out her mother's affects, Lo found the letters from Kay that Mimi mentioned and read a less censored version of the strife Katherine was going through.

In any case, Lo closed the green shutters on the windows of the little Bay cottages, locked the French doors with the big iron 'skeleton key,' and returned to her big empty house in New Orleans to wait. Lola waited, the cottages waited, and Tarzan Oaks waited. They waited for the next generation. They waited for Katherine and her three small children.

Tarzan Oaks survives the centuries as it looks out on the Bay of St. Louis whose waves wash ashore only twenty feet from the giant oak.

The log cabin outside Hamburg where Mimi grew up before marrying Charles Magee, the traveling schoolteacher.

Papa App stands in the doorway of his shoe store in St. Louis, Missouri, where he married Mimi and adopted Lola.

Mimi stands in the doorway of her shop in Bay St. Louis. The Schmidt's summer corner cottage, at left, would be where her granddaughter, Katherine, would raise her three children.

Chapter Three
KATHERINE

Having survived my birth, Katherine was committed to the task of getting on with life. Having survived several life and death struggles in my own life, I think I know exactly how she felt.

My greatest physical challenge later in my adult life was surviving an explosion. As I stood in the middle of my two bedroom frame house which had accidentally filled with escaped natural gas which accidentally ignited, I covered my face with my hands and peered through my fingers for an avenue of escape. I looked through the living room to see the air on fire and the dust particles in the air sparkling like the sparklers we used to light as children during Halloween. I looked into the bathroom to see the paint blistering and peeling from the walls. I looked into the kitchen and saw the plastic appliances melting like hot wax and spilling their bubbling liquid contents all around them.

The arson squad said it took only a fraction of a second to ignite, but I think it took about three seconds before I heard what to me sounded like the muted thud of a base drum emanating from my abdomen. However, the explosion broke windows on the USC Medical Campus a block away and some nearby residents wondered if it was the commencement of World War III.

As I stood amid the sooty remains of my home and belongings, I was afraid to remove my hands from my face. I realized what had happened and that my body was galvanized with pain, but I was afraid to open my eyes and assess my injuries. I decided that if I uncovered my eyes and saw any part of my insides laying on the floor in front of me, I would simply lay down beside them and give up my life. I uncovered my eyes and looked down at my feet to discover my body, though burned and bleeding, was intact. My polyester shirt and tie had melted, my suit was covered with vertical rents through which some blood oozed, and my hands looked like barbecued pork, charcoal black with bleeding pink cracks in them. What I didn't know was that what little remained of my hair was still burning or melted into a surrealistic plastic sculpture, that 25% of my body was covered with 2nd and 3rd degree burns, and that I would look forward to six weeks in a burns ward, three major skin graft surgeries over a painful eight month period, and two years of being an outpatient.

All I knew at that moment was that I had made a commitment one way or the other before I uncovered my eyes. As far as I knew, my body was salvageable and, for better or for worse, I needed it to fulfill the many things I still wanted to do in life.

In those seconds before the explosion, I had sent urgent mental messages to any and all deities, all my departed relatives, and any positive forces who could sympathize with my desire to realize the many unfulfilled things in my life. Whether I survived with or without their assistance, I had already made the appeal, I had already made the deal, and, being still in one piece, I was committed to life.

I ran across what I suddenly realized was the collapsed roof of the house. I ran across what I sadly recognized was my beautiful grand piano blown 35 feet out into the front yard. And I ran in the direction I knew was the hospital. I knew it would not be easy, but I knew it was the only way to move forward, it was the only way to continue with my life.

I suspect Katherine felt much like that as the days slipped by and she and her newborn continued to rally to life. After a few weeks, her first two children were bringing her hand made Valentine cards. Shortly thereafter, the children were caught up in their first experience of the Mardi Gras. Finally, Easter seemed to symbolize the arrival of Spring and the commitment to a new life.

As soon as she could walk, finances were the first order of business. Katherine had been trained in the niceties of life, all the cultural education her father's wealth could provide. But, in the depression, there was not a ready market for such talents. Playing the violin and teaching arts and crafts were always things 'Miss Katherine' had provided as a community service. At a time when most people's resources could not fully provide the barest necessities of life, subsidizing the arts for the sake of their children's education or Miss Katherine's survival was not high on the list of priorities.

After I was grown, I heard about her first attempt to seek employment in New Orleans while Lola stayed with the children in the Bay. Katherine answered a classified ad for a masseuse to give 'local massage.' Clinically speaking, a local massage is intended to provide therapy for a specific limb or joint or area that is troubled. Katherine's interview seemed legitimate enough to her, the well appointed establishment and crisply uniformed personnel seemed suitably impressed with her training and experience which had been acquired to enable her eldest son to overcome his handicaps.

She was surprised and greatly relieved to be hired after the briefest of interviews, given a freshly starched uniform, and sent to a room to meet her first 'patient.' A nice conservative looking middle aged man lay face up on the massage table dressed only in a towel laid loosely over his midriff. He seemed a little nervous and disinclined to respond to her entrance or ensuing queries. She inquired as to the nature of his ailment; did he have a sore back, an arthritic joint, or a limb recently removed from a cast?

His response was to fling aside the towel covering his groin. Katherine retrieved the towel and surreptitiously replaced it over his body, all the time questioning as to the 'locality' of his need for massage. Again he removed the towel. Again she replaced it. Finally the man rose up on his elbows, glared at her, and said, "Listen, girlie, I'm on my lunch hour. If you don't get me up and off and out of here, I'm going to be late getting back to work."

As naive as Katherine was, it finally dawned on her that the man was not as much out of place as she was. The expression on the face of her interviewers took on a new meaning as they pressed her on her experience with 'locals,' a term which to the illegitimate massage parlor of those days meant assisted masturbation or a 'hand job,' if you prefer.

Katherine burst into tears and the man suddenly became very solicitous and apologetic, eventually getting an explanation from her between her tears and sobs. He, in turn, felt obliged to explain that he lived with his mother, could not marry because of her dependence on him, and was deathly afraid of disease. Only because of these circumstances did he employ these services on a weekly basis. He insisted she accept the usual two dollar fee which the management would be expecting from her as she left the room.

Katherine explained to the proprietor who became enraged that a regular customer had been inconvenienced, and, as Katherine left the establishment, she heard the customer berating the proprietor for placing such an innocent girl in such an embarrassing position. Of course, we'll never know if the gentleman got back to work on time.

Katherine did ultimately derive a meager addition to her almost non-existent income from her labors as a masseuse, but she was her own employer, her 'parlor' was one end of our living room in the Bay, and her clients mostly the more affluent and overweight ladies of the town who believed someone else could remove their flab without them having to exert any effort.

I received my earliest lessons in anatomy as a toddler crawling around the living room floor while Katherine heaved and pummeled those large pink bodies on the homemade massage table covered in black oilcloth. Their glistening torsos reeked of 'oil of wintergreen' and they groaned and moaned while Katherine sweated and strained over them until the armpits of her homemade black and white satin uniform were soaking wet.

Her accessories sometimes looked like instruments of torture and frequently elicited appropriate sounds from her clients. One had multiple two inch diameter white rubber balls rotating on a steel framework terminating in a black enamel handle. Once I rolled it over my babyfat abdomen and it pinched the hell out of me.

I don't remember how long her career as a lady's masseuse lasted, but I know that heavy massage table lived at the far end of our living room for many years throughout my infancy. Perhaps I am fortunate that most of the ladies were not too attractive and that I was perhaps too young to be stimulated by them, because I didn't grow up to be a massage parlor devotee or get turned on by oil of wintergreen. Perhaps the worst influence it had on me was manifested in my predilection for hiding my diapers and running around the neighborhood in the buff.

There was an auto repair shop across the street from our house operated by a stocky man named Mr. Cranky who reminded me of Alley Oop, the caveman in the comic strips of the day. Usually it was Mr. Cranky who would find me bare assed playing amidst the greasy auto parts in his shop. Katherine and Lo's search for the missing infant was most often resolved by the appearance of Mr. Cranky in all his cro-magnon glory, his greasy overalls, and his visored cap that came down to his black bushy eyebrows which formed a continuous line across his low forehead. With one hairy hand he held onto the hand of cherubic little me, and in the other hairy hand he held my discarded diapers.

Another of Katherine's home industries in those early days in the Bay was that of dance teacher. This was probably concurrent with the massage clientele, because I remember that the massage table always had to be moved out of the way when dance class turned our living room into a dance studio. I suspect the dance classes lasted a few more years, however, because I was probably beginning to be old enough to be turned on by the sight of all those nubile nymphet figures flitting around the living room.

At any rate, I have been conscious throughout my adult life of an especial attraction to dance in all forms, dancers of the female gender, and even rehearsal dance apparel when worn by my ladyfriends. Perhaps the dance classes also contributed to my liberality regarding gender orientation and homosexuality.

Boys were never brave enough to take ballet lessons then as the media had never informed them that a ballerina works harder and has more agility than a football player. Male dance roles fell to the taller or thinner or most boyish looking girls. Their breasts, if any, were tied down with linen bandages, their hair cut in a short gamin style, and their clown or military or Fred Astaire type costumes were dedicated to art as they would never have another use for them.

At first they would blush and giggle and break up at the mirrored sight of themselves as males. Then they'd blush even further when coached to give the dynamic responses of a male to their female partners. I think that in Katherine's mind it was considered easy and innocent for a young girl to assume a boy's image and behavior.

As I look at old photos of a teenage Katherine

dressing in male drag on many occasions, it always appears in the context of good clean fun that was popular in that day. She appears as a Tom Sawyer type scaring little girls with frogs and slopping the pigs. At times she was a World War I soldier driving cars and smoking cigarettes in a brash and racy manner. On many occasions she was the elegant bridegroom of a male bride in drag, sometimes with an entire bridal party in drag. On the back of one of these photos she noted, "Don't I make a handsome man," and indeed she did; extremely handsome and extremely convincing.

I considered one photo to be quite revealing. It was one of the very few costume photos in which Katherine was the bride, and her father was the groom. On some of the photos of her in drag, other family members wrote "Our Boy" or "Our Son" or "One of the neighborhood boys." It seems obvious to me that Katherine wanted to be the son her father wanted but never had, but equally obvious that her love for him was ardent and not passionate.

Once married, Katherine strove to be as feminine as all the famous femme fatales of her day. In the many photos of her with her young dance students in the Bay, Katherine was always in the feminine role, usually costumed in something gossamer a la Isadora Duncan. I never found a photo of her in male drag past her teenage years.

Nor do I think the boyish looking teenage girls who partnered the other girls around our living room dance studio ever suffered from the experience. It was an acceptable way for them to practice the courting rituals of our society, and whether a particular student was bowing or curtsying, kissing or being kissed, it was all part of a fantasy in which she imagined herself as the feminine object of desire, regardless of the role she played.

.

The cash transactions of Katherine's massage

and dance clients seemed to always involve clinking coins, almost never the soft rustle of paper money. At times it hardly seemed worth the effort, much less the occasional medical consequences. On those occasions, clients would have to be rescheduled because mother was ill. I knew the illness involved hemorrhaging because at those times her bed sheets were not washed on the corrugated washboard and washtub in the backyard, but rather in the bathtub where neighbors could not see the massive bloodstains. She would remain bedridden for days and sometimes there would be a frightening urgent request for one of the children to run the five short blocks to Doctor Horton's office to see if he could attend her.

During the summer we could count on about three months rent at $25 a month from the cottage next door. Of course, that was not without its complications. Lo was in the habit of completely furnishing her rentals, despite the frequent disastrous consequences.

I remember as a small child accompanying her on her shopping trips to furnish her New Orleans apartments. We went to the auction houses on Camp Street in downtown New Orleans where bidding often started at a nickel for items of furniture, draperies, kitchen appliances, and you name it right down to small lots of chipped dishes and mismatched silverware. Lo actually furnished her apartments with everything including bed linens and towels, and, more often than not, she was royally ripped off.

The wildest story about terrible tenants concerned some 'Yankees' who wintered in one of her beautifully furnished apartments, but were so cheap and so insensitive that they broke up the antique furnishings to use as fuel in the fireplace. They left a vindictive note on the mantlepiece complaining that they had been "cheated" by stories of how warm the winters were in the sunny South, only to find that they actually had to build fires in the fireplace to keep warm some of the nights.

The little rental cottage in the bay never suffered from quite such outrageous tenants, but it was an annual chore to touch up the exterior with green and white paints that seemed as thin as whitewash (maybe they were), and refurnish the interior with whatever had been broken or stolen by the previous tenants, or borrowed by our household during the untenanted part of the year. Then, at the end of the summer, the mattresses would usually have to be deloused and the kitchen inevitably subjected to a thorough cockroach extermination campaign.

Transient tenants would never keep a kitchen clean or take any precautions to keep from attracting roaches, and, in that climate, la cucaracha was at least three inches long and capable of flying the full length of any room in those little cottages.

In addition to the summer rental income, there were other virtues to the summer season. I remember my first family visit to Tarzan Oaks and the combination of joy and fear with which I rode on my mother's shoulders into the warm salty waters of the Bay. In time I managed to become a good swimmer and an eternal lover of that magical ribbon of sand where the land meets the sea. On many shores around this globe I have listened to the hypnotic sounds of the surf, written the secrets of my heart in the ever changing sands, and shared moments of meditation, revelation, and inspiration with the elements.

The summer seashore also brought us foodstuffs that were unseasonable or just too cold to go out and catch in the winter. We were lousy fishermen, but even the poorest fisherman could not help but come up with something from the fishy cornucopia of that Bay. We had no boat in which to go out and catch the marlin, swordfish, red snapper, and speckled trout in the deeper waters. We had no kerosene pole lanterns and spears to look for flounders after sunset when they slept in the shallow waters. And we had no costly hand-knit throw nets to fling so gracefully like a dancer's skirts into the reedy waters at the edge of the Bay where the small tasty shrimp abound.

      Instead, we settled for the croakers and whitefish that were willing to accept our humble earthworms as bait in shallow water, even though the croakers and whitefish were considered good only for bait themselves. If we were confident or desperate enough to borrow someone's crab nets, we would walk out on the two mile wooden auto bridge that crossed the Bay along Highway 90, and lower the nets the tremendous distance into the water, praying that the string would not break and lose the net forever. After 15 or 20 minutes, an infinitely patient and steady slow raising of the string would bring the net to the surface of the water and possibly reveal a crab feeding on the bait in the middle of the basket shaped net. As soon as he was visible, it was a race between you and the crab to see if you could get the net up on the bridge before the crab could crawl out of it. Most of the time we lost the race, but we succeeded often enough to augment our protein poor diet with the delicacy of boiled crab once in a while.

      Summer also meant that lesser fare could be enhanced by our mother's famous 'Tarzan lunches.' These were nothing but common brown bag lunches, usually consisting of bologna or peanut butter and jelly sandwiches, with the occasional added treat of fruit or candy. But, and it was a very big 'but,' the bags were painted or appliqued with cutouts of lions and tigers and elephants and bears, and they were hidden in the limbs of Tarzan Oaks or the fig and pecan trees of our backyard. We were obliged to stalk these prey with spears or bow and arrow fashioned from the saplings growing in our backyard, and each 'hunter' was allowed only one 'kill' with the admonition that one never kills more than one can eat. My brother was always tactfully blind to the 'prey' hidden in the lower branches that I could reach, and he even refrained from finding his own lunch until the two smaller children had stumbled upon theirs.

But periodically the trees grew bare, the waters of the Bay grew cold, and we were hard pressed to keep wood in the fireplace, much less food in the cupboard. My brother and sister grew to hate bologna, the most affordable meat in our diet, although I still enjoy it to this day. The thing I couldn't stand was creamed fish on toast. The least expensive canned meat was a small tin of 'fish flakes' which Katherine would stretch into four portions by serving in a white sauce over toast.

The only other meat I remember was liver, which in those days was considered 'pet food.' I remember Lo giving me three nickels and telling me to ask the butcher for "fifteen cents worth of liver for our cat, please." I reluctantly went to Scharff's Grocery on Main Street and asked the butcher, Mr. Noto, for "fifteen cents worth of liver for our cat, please," and suffering that brief pause as he stared into my eyes to assure me he knew full well we were destitute enough to eat animal entrails.

Hunger itself is just another physical pain, like being cut or burned, only the disfigurement is not as immediate or overt. The outer stomach lining shrinks faster than the inner stomach lining causing wrinkles in the interior surface, which in turn cause 'hunger pangs.' When the interior lining shrinks equally, the wrinkles and pain go away, and you simply become listless and depressed.

Being hungry is something more than that, however, something very difficult to explain to the uninitiated. It is a state of mind, an attitude of frustration and then resignation, like being the wrong color or speaking the wrong language in a foreign country. You haven't arrived at it by choice, there's nothing you can do about it or you would have already done it, and you have no alternative but to play a waiting game to see if your physical and emotional reserves will outlast the enforced fasting period.

It's amazing how many things you can do with stale bread. You can cube it, put milk and sugar over it, and tell yourself it's the latest new breakfast cereal. If you have an egg, you can try to squeak eight or ten slices of French Toast through a watery batter and dust them with cinnamon and sugar because we could rarely afford molasses. If you have more than one egg and enough sugar, you can make bread pudding.

But how do you turn stale bread into meat? Brown flour gravy is made from a 'rue.' You add flour to a small amount of melted fat in a skillet over a low flame until the flour becomes scorched. Then you add black chicory coffee slowly until the flour thickens to the right amount. Season it with salt and pepper and pour it over a slice of stale bread on a plate. The final trick is to imagine it is a steak or a slice of ham or turkey as you eat it.

There were times when even the brown flour gravy ran out and the last of the stale bread had the mold scraped off of it before it found a home amid the wrinkles in our stomach lining. Then Katherine had to suffer the inevitable question "why" from her youngest.

"We are going to bed early tonight, children."

"But why, mother?"

"Because there's no wood for the fire and no food for dinner."

"But why, mother?"

"I don't know, honey. I just don't know."

As we would try to concentrate on sleep, sometimes the incessant sound of the crickets would suddenly grow silent, and we would hear Katherine's sobs muffled into her pillow trying to spare us her regrets, pain, and fears, and we would do the same.

Katherine saw her children suffer the combined effects of rickets and malnutrition. She saw them succumb to scarlet fever, whooping cough, and all the worst of children's diseases to which their undernourished bodies had no resistance. She reasoned that she was at fault. She had made a poor choice in a husband. She had not been able to turn him into a good parent. And now she was the one unable to provide an adequate home while everyone else stood around waiting for her to totally fail before they would do anything.

It must have been a cold winter's night during those first few years in the Bay that Katherine came to this guilt ridden conclusion, because it was the unlikely weather that caused the motorist to notice her at the middle of the two mile bridge across the Bay. She must have made a dramatic sight. A beautiful woman in expensive clothes, be they ever so worn and outdated, moving with painful slowness against the drizzling wind and the unhappy goal she had in mind.

She was weak with hunger, the cold damp weather made her arthritis almost crippling, and she was suffering from 'female' complications that only surgery could alleviate. She had convinced herself that, upon her death, her mother, sister, and wealthy friends would adopt and provide for her children far better than she could. She hated the cold and feared the thought of drowning, but could think of no other means of accomplishing her deed.

I suspect it was Mimi who watched over her granddaughter that night and slowed her steps as the motorist made his way into town to report the strange apparition he had seen on the bridge. Surely there was some guardian angel who insured that the motorists tale fell upon Dr. Horton's ears, although the good doctor did not need any prompting to know who the girl on the bridge was. I only know that years later I was told the details of that night to reassure me of the humanity beneath that old man's gruff exterior.

Dr. Horton probably 'cussed' or, at the very least, 'fumed' as he tried to crank start his temperamental old Model T Ford coupe on that cold wet night. Neither was it easy to negotiate through the mists on that rickety old wooden bridge which shuddered each time its pilings were buffeted by high waves.

Finally, the yellow glow of his headlamps barely revealed her shivering figure bent over the railing at the deep channel in the center of the bridge. The wind and water kept her from recognizing his barking voice until he repeated himself.

"Katherine, get in this car, you silly girl."

Katherine shielded her eyes from the headlights, then turned back to the railing. "I'm all right, Dr. Horton. Please leave me alone."

The chatter of the Model T's engine played a staccato counterpoint to the wind and rain, and a brief silence took the edge off of Dr. Horton's voice. "Come here, child."

Katherine lifted a grimly smiling face to the wind as raindrops camouflaged and washed away her tears. "Really, it's okay. I know what I'm doing." Katherine moved a few feet away and sat on the lower rung of the railing. Her arthritis had thwarted her earlier effort to climb the railing. Now, as she sat beneath it, she looked behind her and wondered if she could fall backwards through the railing.

Dr. Horton exited the car and moved toward her. "Katherine?" He stopped when she leaned slightly backward and stared at him threateningly. "So, you know what you're doing, eh, Katherine?"

She looked down into the water. "I know that what I'm doing is in everyone's best interest."

"In the best interest of your children to lose their mother, to be separated, to be raised by strangers?"

Katherine stared at the churning sea. "They'd be with their family and god parents."

Dr. Horton snorted. "An aging widow and an old maid who knows nothing about boys? And even if the infant's godparents do happen to be millionaires, ain't no amount of money gonna make that woman human, much less a mother. Dammit, Katherine, you're the best mother any child could hope to have, and you'd deny your talents to your own children?"

Katherine spoke in a whisper to the water below. "It's in everyone's best interest."

The old man hobbled a little closer. "What you say, girl?"

Katherine turned and angrily raised her voice. "I said, it's in everyone's best interest."

Dr. Horton leaned over her. "Well, child, it's not in my best interest."

She wiped the rainwater from her forehead with the back of her hand and looked up at him perplexed. "Your best interest? What do you mean?"

He threw up his hands. "I mean, how long do you think I'd last down there trying to fish you outta that water?"

She frowned at him. "You couldn't. You've got a bum leg."

He leaned down again, resting his hands on his knees. "You don't think that would stop me. You know me well enough to know I'm just like you. We wouldn't give up on life, ours or anyone else's, until we had spent our last ounce of strength and our last breath trying. Would we?"

For a long time tears streamed down Katherine's face faster than the raindrops could wash them away, until finally Dr. Horton said, "Well, are we gonna jump or are we gonna go home, 'cause we couldn't get any wetter down there than we're getting up here?"

Katherine threw her arms around him so hard he almost lost his balance, but she held him too tight to let him fall. Then, wiping the tears from her eyes, she let him help her into the old Model T which was still chugging away.

12-year-old Katherine plays a bride as her father, Will, proposes.

Katherine plays groom to male family friend who plays bride.

14-year-old Katherine *(left)* and girlfriend *(right)* dress up as World War I soldiers pretending to smoke cigarettes.

Katherine teaches dance in Bay St. Louis where her all-girl class obliges tallest and thinnest girls to assume male roles.

Original John Churchill Chase cartoon from 3/9/34 *New Orleans Item* depicting President Franklin Delano Roosevelt (FDR) looking back on his first year in office which began at the height of 'The Great Depression.' He took office 43 days after the author was born, led the nation out of the depression with work programs like the WPA and the CCC, and took America's head out of the sand regarding isolationism and the immanence of World War II. He was the only American President to serve more than 2 terms. John Churchill Chase was a person with a disability and, though the public was unaware that FDR had polio, Chase depicted him with a cane.

Chapter Four
STATEN ISLAND

Things did not improve overnight, but, ever so slowly, they did improve. The nights we went to bed without a meal were fewer. The long periods of brown flour gravy on bread for supper grew shorter. And more and more eggs and milk and chicken crept into our diet, spinoffs from the barter of Dr. Horton's rural patients.

Dr. Horton didn't need a nurse, but, for a while, Katherine played nurse in his drab office in that drab grey building on Main Street. She learned how to stitch up our minor cuts with needle and thread, how to make topical unguents from iodine and petroleum jelly, and how to make cough syrup from lemon, honey, and whiskey. She learned the practicality and humbuggery of home remedies, Indian remedies, and the poetic license of dispensing Muscatel wine from medicinal bottles labeled "sleeping medicine" and Port wine from medicinal bottles labeled "blood tonic."

Katherine learned that a country doctor is much more than a general practitioner, at least in Dr. Horton's case. He was a veterinarian, a psychiatrist, a psychologist, a marriage counselor, a politician, a little bit of a quack, and a lot of playing God and Robin Hood. He charged the rich hypochondriacs outrageously for his gruff bedside manner and placebo sugar pills, then he worked like a Trojan for the poor who could only pay him with chickens and eggs which he would in turn give to Katherine and other needy people like ourselves. If there is a heavenly judgment, I am sure he can be forgiven the rare moments when he had to decide who went without food or services, who had to live, and who had to die.

Dr. Horton was probably the communication link

between Katherine's sense of guilt and Lola's naivete concerning the dire circumstances we were in. Ultimately, Katherine, her mother Lola, and her sister 'Aunt Thelma,' thrashed out the realities of the situation. It was decided that Katherine and the three children would go to live with Aunt Thelma in her big house on Staten Island, New York.

Aunt Thelma bought us a new 1939 Plymouth to drive to New York, and most of the driving was done by Bob Bumgarner who had long wanted to be Katherine's beau. In the year prior to going to Staten Island, friends in New Orleans had tried to get the two of them together, but I don't think the chemistry worked for Katherine. After the experience of her marriage, she was sexually turned off, and Bob Bumgarner's gentle manliness and sincerity could still not cut through the ice.

Bob was originally from Virginia and, at the time he first came to Bay St. Louis to meet Katherine, he was operating a 'horsewire' from a hotel room in New Orleans, telegraphing race results to bookies. He persevered in a platonic friendship with her before, during, and after the trip to New York where he became a roomer in Aunt Thelma's house and a telegrapher for Merril, Lynch, Pierce, Fenner, and Bean.

The auto trip from the Gulf Coast to New York was my first great cross-country travel adventure. My brother and sister had been back and forth between Canada and New Orleans, but my travels had been confined to the sixty miles between the Bay and New Orleans and one brief visit to Hamburg, the little place outside Natchez where Mimi was born and raised.

We loaded the trunk, then the top of the car, and finally packed the back seat full enough to make a level platform where we three kids spent most of our time playing Monopoly, Chinese Checkers, and Mah Jong with the genuine ivory and bamboo playing pieces that fit in their hand carved wooden case. Of course, A.J., the eternal bookworm, read most of the time.

We had seen big cities before, the world's second largest river (the Mississippi), and been across the world's highest suspension bridge (the Huey P. Long bridge spanning the Mississippi River) and the world's longest bridge (the 40 mile long Lake Ponchatrain Causeway), both just outside of New Orleans. So we were not exactly country bumpkins.

But the mountain ranges of the Great Smokies and the Appalachians were an altogether new experience for me. I remember realizing for the first time that the environs of cartoon characters like Li'l' Abner and Snuffy Smith were drawn from life and not pure imagination. And, indeed, our car crept up narrow winding mountain roads with little or no road signs or markings or guard rails to protect us from the sheer precipices overlooking dizzying heights that made our teeth grind and our hair stand on end.

Even our little dog, Schnapsie, was as scared as we were. A rat terrier who had been given to us by Aunt Mary before she went to the Confederate Old Folks Home at Beauvoir, we had named him after the dachshund portrayed in the comic strip *Schnapsie And The Colonel*. Fortunately, Schnapsie was a tiny little thing, otherwise he might not have been included in that muchly over-packed and over-peopled car on such a long trip.

Katherine occupied us with word games and singing songs and advice designed to prepare us for life in a big city and living with our unmarried childless Aunt Thelma. We pretty much got the idea that other adults did not have to tolerate anything from we children and we must be on our best behavior for we were, more or less, going to be on probation.

Thelma Inez Schmidt had inherited her share of the family's brains and talent. As a little girl she had been a dance prodigy and danced with the celebrated theatrical and vaudeville personalities and companies of the day, but only as a socialite ingénue and never as a paid professional. She later studied piano seriously for the concert stage, but her mother found that career unacceptable. She had also inherited her mother's round face and, despite Thelma's petiteness, her mother's mesomorphic body.

Between Lola's over-protectiveness and Thelma's cupie doll roundness, Aunt Thelma was not a hot item on the marriage market and, in her twenties, seemed destined for old maidhood.

Upon graduating from St. Agnes Academy, a Catholic 'Musical Conservatory' in Memphis, Tennessee, shortly after World War I, Thelma became a novitiate and began to prepare herself for a life of service as a nun. I do not know if it was her family or her own decision, but, in time, she changed her mind and left for New York City where, I'm sure she felt, she would finally be free of Lola's apron strings.

In her early forties by the time we joined her on Staten Island, Aunt Thelma had become a successful executive in the RCA Overseas Office which, in part, involved telegraphy of stock quotations via the Trans-Atlantic cable with Europe. Her two story home in the Huguenot District of Staten Island had five bedrooms, two baths, a beautiful grand piano, central heating, a strange thing called a 'basement,' and a front yard with three terraced levels.

Thelma loved the theater and her circle of friends included the noted painter Paul Scofield and other illuminaries of the artistic world of that day. I remember being dragged to 'avant garde' cocktail parties in 'moderne' apartments that overlooked Manhattan from dizzying heights. The ladies mostly looked like Aunt Jolan, our family friend 'jet-setter' from New Orleans who bounced around the world before there were jets to get her there. Their bodies were garbed in clothing that was skin tight from the waist to below the knee, their shapely legs always encased in shiny black hose, and their heavily painted horsy faces surmounted by either turbans or berets.

The men all looked like penguins in loose clothing, their gender accented by the shortness of their cigarette holders compared to those of the ladies. One wondered about the occasional man with a long or decorous cigarette holder.

Thelma was a natural for their company. Her intelligence, talent, social graces, and affluence were on a par with them, yet her looks did not compete with the women and her profession did not compete with the artists. Her compassion allowed her to educate the 'nouveau riche,' and her background made her a charter member of the establishment.

Professionally she had shrewdness, strength, drive, and determination. Socially she had taste, grace, warmth, and a surprising wit. In these circles she was a late bloomer, a hesitant adventurer with just enough of the naivete still about her. After all, what fun is it to go slumming unless someone in the group is still shockable.

As the poor relations, we were infrequent well mannered props in this 'high life.' On the rides to the city or Scofield's riverfront apartment overlooking Manhattan, the 'L' (elevated railroad) ran through the worst imaginable slums. As the train stopped at each station, you'd often be looking directly into the windows of tenements where scowling screaming people communicated their frustration and depression in drinking, violence, and a variety of languages and accents. I would think how ironic that there, but for the grace of Aunt Thelma, went we. For, had we been raised in New York City as poor as we had been on the Gulf Coast, those tenements adjacent to the 'L' would surely have been our fate.

But fate had been kind to us and we had been enriched by the natural beauty of the surroundings in which we grew up and the ideals of the generations that had preceded us.

Staten Island was, at that time, a small community like Bay St. Louis in some ways. There was plenty of space and no pollution in terms of air, water, people, or noise, as opposed to the insufferability of New York City. The backyard bordered on some woods which abounded in blackberries. There was only one neighbor adjacent to us and, because of the wooded rolling hills, there were no other houses in sight, as far as the range of a six-year-old could tell.

Two of my lifelong interests found their earliest seeds there. One was photography, the hobby of the Capes, the childless couple next door. I was fascinated by their fireplace which Mr. Cape had built with boulders from the surrounding area. The center stone was mammoth, and I delighted in hearing him tell how he conned some of his dinner guests into helping him put the stone into place after he had plied them with too much liquor to refuse. He would re-enact the role of each of his drunken friends, and I would applaud his performance no matter how many times I had heard the story.

Mr. Cape was an architect and a fairly serious photographer. He took a high-key picture of me that was a study in whites; white saddle shoes, short white pants, white shirt, my cherubic white face, my white cornsilk hair blowing in the wind, all against a white snowy background. He titled it *Honey Chile,* because the adult women in our family usually addressed a six-year-old as 'honey,' and it won him first prize in a local contest.

Once he let me into the inner sanctum of his basement darkroom. I was in awe of the darkened room filled with red light, much less the magic of seeing images appear on a blank sheet of paper immersed in trays of weird smelling solutions.

He gave me a few brief explanations as he made exposures on the paper with his enlarger, cautioning me not, under any circumstances, to touch or jar anything during the exposures. As I moved closer to peer at the mysterious negative image of myself as a black boy with black hair and clothes against a black background, I accidentally bumped the enlarger baseboard. Mr. Cape yelled at me sharply and, cursing, removed the paper from the easel and crumpled it into a ball. I hesitated a few very brief moments to compose myself, then, embarrassed, left his darkroom never to return. I could hear Mrs. Cape chiding him for frightening me, but, more than my concern whether or not Mr. Cape was mad at me, I was enthralled with my first introduction to the magical process of photography.

The other magical discovery in life was my Aunt Thelma's piano. That beautiful six foot Weber full grand piano had been bought for her brand new by her father when she was a small child just before the turn of the century in New Orleans. She had poured a lifetime of hopes and regrets into it, and it was a symbol as well as a friend to her. We children had been admonished never to touch it upon pain of being boiled in oil.

The only musical instrument in our home up to that time had been Katherine's violin. We had been allowed to touch it, to feel its body vibrate as she played it the way she would let deaf children touch it when they were present in the rural churches in which she sometimes performed. On rare occasions she would, I think, test our potential interest by letting us hold the violin under our chins and stroke the bow across the strings which, despite her instructions, never produced anything indistinguishable from a cat in pain.

Aunt Thelma's piano, however, had a keyboard with which even the family cat, who was allowed to touch it more than we were, could produce beautiful sounds. It sat with black satin elegance amid the corner windows at one end of the sizable dining room, and I discovered that, sitting beneath it and holding down the sustaining pedal, I could hear the wind from the windows play through the strings like a glissando on a harp sending chills up my spine.

It was painful to hear untalented hands touch this beautiful instrument and produce a grating discordance that turned it into a primitive rhythm instrument. I resented the license of adults who were allowed to so profane its' noble design while I was not allowed to even touch it.

But when Aunt Thelma sat down to play the classics, particularly when she thought she was alone and didn't know I was watching, it was obvious she was transported by the exquisite sounds her chubby little hands wrought from its ivory keys. I imagined she sat at the controls of a celestial spaceship, moving our house and all within it through the gliding spiraling paths of heaven.

It would be many years before I was ever allowed to touch this piano. I would write my first songs on it. Twenty-five years after residing in Staten Island, I would inherit it from my Aunt and it would travel back and forth with me between New Orleans and Hollywood several times before it would ultimately expire in the explosion that almost took my life.

One of my first short stories was titled "The Mistress," a first person narrative that read like a passionate woman's account of her many male and female lovers, only to be revealed as the soul of this piano recalling its response to the hands and hearts of all who had touched its keys with love.

In the latter years of that piano's life, my piano tuner in Hollywood had been Mr. Forgy. Mr. Forgy looked like Mr. Gipetto from Walt Disney's Pinocchio. He had become a piano tuner after returning from World War I, and had made his toolkit at that time with its hand carved recesses for each and every tool.

He was a favorite of many world renown pianists and the principal piano tuner for many of the radio, television, and motion picture studios through the years.

Like Dr. Horton, he charged according to ability to pay, and he tuned my piano for a fifth of what he charged concert artists.

The first time he worked on my piano, he ran the back of his index finger across the keyboard, caressed the corner of its ebony case, then looked at me and said, "You realize, son, you ain't got no thumpbox here."

That made me flash back to 1939 on Staten Island and the principal adult whose insensitive hands had turned this piano into a 'thumpbox' each time he touched, or rather pounded, its keys. His name was Bob Morris, a fellow telegrapher Bob Bumgarner brought home from the brokerage. Mr. Morris took one look at Aunt Thelma's well appointed home, and he knew when he smelled a good thing.

Bob Morris became a roomer also, and eventually squeezed Bob Bumgarner out of the household. He got Bob Bumgarner drunk one night and convinced him he should be aggressive with Katherine. Poor Bob Bumgarner tried to crawl in bed with Katherine and was promptly invited to leave the house.

Bob Morris was originally from Appalachia and, in looks, reminded me a little of Hoagy Carmichael, the songwriter. He was a conniver, an exploiter, and had a heavy hand with the bottle, the piano, and the ladies. He taught my fourteen-year old brother to drink, he made unwelcome passes at my mother, and he ultimately set his sights for Aunt Thelma who obviously held the purse strings and was the most susceptible to his rustic charms.

Bob Morris was the thorn in our side at home. At school, we all had more than a few thorns adjusting to a new society. It was my first introduction to the outside world, and it was not entirely a smooth one.

At school I began writing with my left hand, which caused the faculty to force me to write with my right hand, which caused me to write backwards with my right hand, and sometimes caused me to write simultaneously in opposite directions with both hands, but in the wrong directions.

Katherine, who had read more about child psychology than most of the teachers and counselors who got involved, tried to explain to them about the left side of the brain and the right side of the brain and how she did not want me to be forced to conform at the expense of repressing my creativity, etc. etc. etc.. The harder she tried to explain, the harder they leaned on me, until I began to feel there was a conspiracy to keep me from being one of the 'group.'

The conspiracy theory was compounded by the other children. Not the ones in my class, but the older bullies who, during recess and lunch, extorted any money or food or valuables I had on me, or simply pounded on me for the sadistic pleasure. The black bullies explained their right to terrorize me was because I was from Mississippi, but I didn't buy that because I had experienced no precedent of segregation nor was I aware of any class struggle such as they alluded to. Besides, their technique and results were the same as the white bullies who wasted no time on such rationalizations.

I discovered my sister and brother went through similar problems adjusting to school there. Fortunately for my brother, the first bully who tried the 'Mississippi' routine on him received a lucky punch from my brother which sent the boy tumbling down the staircase, never to bother him again. Unfortunately for us little guys, almost everyone in the world was just too big to stand up to.

But, despite school, New York had its compensations. It had more museums than New Orleans, although there seemed to be less paintings of beautiful scenery and pretty half clothed ladies, and a lot more 'modern' art which my six-year-old mind could not interpret, appreciate, nor accept. I'm afraid that in the decades since, my appreciation of modern art has not increased by much.

The 1939 World's Fair was on Long Island with a massive sculpture of a ball and spire as its' symbol. I remember attending it and being mesmerized by the display of a transistor radio circuit encased in a large Lucite brick the size of a shoebox, its' seven quarter sized transistors actually powering a speaker which spoke with a robotic voice comparing this miracle to Dick Tracy's famous though fictional wristwatch radio. For the rest of my school years, my classmates derided the story of such an impossible device.

New York had many other wondrous things. There was the Statue of Liberty (I was afraid to look down), the Chrysler Building (I was afraid to look down), and the Empire State Building (I was afraid to look down, but when I saw King Kong I was proud to have been there). There were restaurants where you could make your own breakfast right at your own table (they charged outrageously for the raw ingredients), restaurants where the waiters were famous for their rudeness and scathing insults to the customers (the customers must have been masochists because they seemed to love it), and restaurants where there were no waiters and all the food was behind little coin operated doors that looked like post office mailboxes (the Automat was not famous for fresh food).

There were elevated railroads (very noisy), subways (scary even then), and the Staten Island Ferry which was worth even going to the doctor's in order to enjoy a round trip ferry ride (ah, the thrill of the sea).

Of course, the biggest plus in our lives on Staten Island was our diet. The kitchen stove burned an invisible gas that came from nowhere and never had to be refilled like our old kerosene stove. It didn't smell like our kerosene stove and it never caught fire or blew up. The kitchen also boasted a genuine refrigerator with a strange looking round thing on top that resembled the Capitol Records building in Hollywood which was designed to resemble a stack of phonograph records. We were allowed to eat any raw vegetables or fruit or drink as much milk as we wanted out of it, and that's not all. There were all kinds of breads and rolls and muffins, and none of them were stale, unless you were six-years-old and didn't understand the natural state of a bagel.

There were strange new things like waffles made in our own waffle iron with a little red jeweled light on top that told you it was working, and real butter and real maple syrup to put on top of them. There were blintzes that made our heavy pancakes look like the poor relations we were, and there was cream cheese and marmalade and all kinds of sweet things to put in them. There was meat at every single supper, and sometimes two and three times a day. More than half the dishes set before us, I had never seen before.

We had arrived in early summer and, by November, we had finally become adjusted to this kitchen of plenty. Proof that we had progressed past the starving child mentality was that we didn't eat every last thing on the Thanksgiving table. Even the major portion of the major sized turkey was left intact with most of its fabulous oyster dressing.

We all retired to the front porch to enjoy the afternoon sun and, after the better part of an hour, our attention was distracted by the appearance of the family cat, the one who sometimes walked across the piano keys to assert her territorial prerogative where I was not allowed. She ambled through the front door by putting all four paws forward, then lifting a hugely swollen abdomen forward a few inches before resting briefly, then repeating the process. Upon investigation, we discovered she had gotten on the table and eaten a tunnel completely through the turkey, stuffing and all. We were seriously concerned about her survival, but sunbathing on the porch for the rest of the day seemed to do the trick, and she lived to set an example for us all of the sins of gluttony.

A.J. was fourteen and, between peer pressure at school and Bob Morris for a role model, he began to smoke and drink. Whether it was the combination of the two or sheer bad luck, his attic room caught fire and, though the rest of the house was spared, our probation now had a black mark on it.

Bob Morris began to court Aunt Thelma with a vengeance, plying her with more liquor than she was used to, groping her on the living room sofa in the company of others, and making enough of a spectacle in the presence of her friends to jeopardize her professional and social image. But Aunt Thelma's romantic delirium made her blind to it all.

War had broken out in Europe, and the Nazi propaganda machine was in high gear in New York City fanning the flames of racism and anti-Semitism. Bob Morris was the perfect type such two valued thinking was designed for, finding it simpler to blame others for his losses and failures in life, and offending Aunt Thelma's Jewish and liberal social and professional peers in the process. But Aunt Thelma was high on love, or what passed for it in Bob's courting rituals.

Katherine tried to communicate to her sister the reality of Bob's drinking, womanizing, and mercenary intentions, but Aunt Thelma's mid-life crisis did not make her receptive to the truth, and Katherine's honesty only served as another black mark on our probation.

Ultimately, Aunt Thelma married Bob Morris and he became 'lord of the manor.' Katherine could not enter the basement laundry room without one of we children to chaperon her. Bob's attempts at 'male bonding' with A.J. kept Katherine constantly worried as to what questionable values A.J. was being exposed. And Bob regarded Katherine as the greatest impediment to parting Aunt Thelma from her money, so he mounted a campaign to split the two sisters.

As the youngest, I was aware of the household tensions, but not the specifics of these intrigues. I was in the midst of my first experience with snow and a white Christmas. Aunt Thelma's Christmas tree had real electric lights on it, some of the bulbs surrounded by star shaped crystals and some in the form of Santa or elves or angels. There was a child's fantasy of chocolate Santas, giant candy canes, and pressed glass jars filled with shiny hard candies of every shape and color. There were exotic new treats like maple sugar candies and guava jelly which came in little wooden boxes with labels burned into the tops.

In addition to the familiar peanuts and pecans, there were walnuts, Brazil nuts, hazelnuts, butter nuts, and a local chestnut which you not only roasted in the open fireplace, but also put into the stuffing of the Christmas roast duck. And, for a finale to the Christmas meal, there was a fun dessert called 'floating island' with white islands of meringue floating in a sea of thin yellow custard. From the perspective of a once hungry child, Aunt Thelma really knew how to live.

Christmas gifts that year were a giant step into the world of consumerism and materialism. There was not one homemade, handmade, or dime store gift in the lot. Even the wrappings were a treasury of metallic papers and satin ribbons that, when salvaged, would fuel our craft projects for years to come.

I felt sorry for the adults who received such meaningless things as sterling service ware, gold jewelry, and cut glass pieces, while we children received such true realities of life as toys and edibles.

My most memorable gift made me, years later, appreciate the final scene of that masterpiece movie, *Citizen Kane*, when the dying tycoon's last thoughts are of his first childhood sled, 'Rosebud.' I don't remember the make of the sled I received that Christmas, 'Flyer' or 'Glider' something or the other, but I remember that sense of elation as I took it out to sample the thrills of Aunt Thelma's three tiered terraced front yard. It was like owning your own roller-coaster.

One's first contact with snow is like that first visit to the ocean or that first view from a cloud topped mountain. It is the trinity of the elements; solid, liquid, and gaseous. Each is an awesome phenomena, helping define the physical parameters of the mortal experience. Each is a sensual and esthetic delight, to be viewed with reverence, and to be immersed and reveled in.

While I had reverently viewed my first snowfall through the window and admired the silent purity with which it erased all evidence of human pollution, the Christmas gift of a sled gave me the means and the license to go out and wallow in its crunchy crystalline reality. My brother and sister and I rutted and checkered the slopes of the front yard until there was no unsullied inch of it to be found. Then we turned our attention to the woods behind the house, reconnoitered and tested every slightest elevation that afforded our sleds any momentum, and ended up at a large pond which now served the neighborhood children as a skating rink with the added novelty of viewing fish frozen beneath its' surface. Ice skating, like roller skating, eluded my sense of balance, so I contented myself with trying to pelt my sister with snowballs as she whizzed by.

I enjoyed my winter wonderland until the cold weather found a chink in my formerly malnourished physical armor and I developed tonsilitis. The surgery provided my first experience with hospitals and anesthesia, and the resulting headaches vied with the intensity of the pain in my throat, neither of which were sufficiently compensated for with the promised diet of ice cream.

Next I became bedridden with double mastoiditis, a potentially fatal infection of the mastoid bone behind both ears. Penicillin and antibiotics had not yet been invented, and the only treatment was to perforate my eardrums and irrigate through the ear canal with warm water channeled through a complicated looking egg-shaped glass valve that was placed in my ear and activated by a carefully manipulated rubber bulb. Every hour for many days, warm water was gently pumped into and sucked out of each ear in turn. With Katherine's tireless ministrations and more than a little luck, I survived.

The doctor's advice was, "These children were raised in a climate which did not instill resistance to northern winters, so return them to a warm climate." This belied the fact that A.J. and Thelma had spent their childhood in Canadian winters, and I later contracted double mastoiditis again in the summer warmth of the Gulf Coast, but the doctor's advice was believable at the time and, perhaps, Katherine felt it was as good as excuse as any to retreat from a war of wills with Bob Morris.

Slightly less than a year after our arrival on Staten Island, we bid our newfound life of luxury goodbye, pointed the 1939 Plymouth southward, and returned to the same problems we had sought to escape.

Thelma Schmidt

as a vaudeville ingenue,

as a St. Agnes novitiate,

as a Wall St. executive.

Thelma Schmidt visits painter Paul Skofield's waterfront studio overlooking the Hudson.

Staten Island wedding party 1939, *(left to right)* Alfred Thomas, groom Bob Morris, Bob Bumgarner, Thelma Thomas, bride Thelma Schmidt Morris, William Thomas, and two unknown lady friends of the family.

Chapter Five
NEW ORLEANS

We returned to New Orleans and a period of transition as Katherine was forced to seek employment and had to leave we children with her mother in Lola's New Orleans apartment house.

Originally, Lo and her husband had raised their children in a house on the corner of Patton and Coliseum Streets, one block from Exposition Boulevard. Actually, Exposition was not a boulevard, rather it was a walkway that bordered the length of Audubon Park from the Mississippi River to St. Charles Boulevard. Patton Street was parallel to and three blocks from the Mississippi River. It was a quiet respectable residential neighborhood and the corner house was a large elegant structure with a massive oak tree beside it.

By the time we returned from Staten Island, Lo had been forced to sell the corner house, which was a rather palatial residence for one elderly woman, and move into one of the five apartments in the apartment house she owned adjacent to the corner house. This was also a wood frame structure, but of more recent vintage and less palatial. Still, it had hardwood floors, high ceilings, coal grate fireplaces, bay windows in the two downstairs apartments, and massive front screen porches on both first and second floors.

Lo lived in the smaller of the two downstairs apartments, and we moved into the larger one. The two apartments were basically laid out the same, a large front room connected to a large dining room via large double sliding doors, then a hallway with a side door and blockaded stairwell to the second floor, the hall leading to a large kitchen and, in our apartment, a medium sized rear bedroom. There was only one bath serving the two downstairs apartments, and it was on our side. My mother and sister took the living room as their bedroom, because there was a hall that connected the front door to both the living and dining rooms. A.J., now a rather introverted moody young man, took the rear bedroom. And I was put in one corner of the large kitchen with folding screens to awkwardly determine my privacy and territoriality.

The upstairs tenants came and went, and I remember relatively few of them, but there was one young couple that lived directly over my head. The Nordic looking young blonde wife was very attractive, childless, and inclined to form a mutual admiration society with me. At eight, I didn't know why I found her attractive, but I did.

I probably attributed it to the fact that she was fascinated by my interest in things mechanical and challenging to my powers of deductive reasoning. She would solicit defunct alarm clocks, cameras, and radios from the neighbors for me and watch with what I can only guess was motherly pride as I meticulously disassembled them, tried to ascertain how they worked, and sometimes even fixed them. She referred to me as her 'boyfriend,' and I bashfully took secret pride in our relationship.

Lo's peers were in the upper middle age group, quietly affluent with 'old money,' and reaching a point in life where her contact with them was not infrequently prompted by attending the funerals of departed friends. The closest family was Uncle Pete, her deceased husband's brother who had taken over the engraving firm for which, it was reluctantly inferred, he had not entirely compensated Lola.

Though not blood relatives, we were somewhat closer to 'Uncle Grady' and his wife, 'Aunt Sadie.' The story goes that Grady was working as a ditch digger when Will Schmidt met him on a muddy New Orleans street. The ditch digger recognized the well dressed and well known Dr. Schmidt, and laid down planks so the respected doctor could traverse the ditch under construction. Regardless to what degree flattery influenced him, the gregarious Will befriended the likeable Irishman, welcomed him and his wife into his home as social equals, and introduced him to influential people who started Grady on a successful executive career.

The greatest turning point in Grady's career came when he was working as a courier in the head offices of the Gulf Oil Company. He was given a sealed document to deliver to the White Truck Company, and, the shrewd minded businessman he was, Grady steamed it open to discover an order for 60 oil trucks. Knowing such an order in those days would dramatically increase White Truck stock values, Grady bought all the stock he could before delivering the order.

He generously called Will to advise him to do likewise, knowing Will was in a financial position to buy far more stock than Grady could afford. Will was in New York at the time, so he called Lola in New Orleans and instructed her to have his lawyer invest every available asset in White Truck Company. The conservative, timid, Lola was afraid of risking the comfort and security she had come to know, and did not relay the instructions to the lawyer. Formerly a shaky company on the verge of bankruptcy, White Truck Company stock soared and made an additional killing when it was bought up by General Motors. Grady became a millionaire almost overnight, and Will never once reproached Lola for her omission that had cost them a fortune.

Sadie was a beautiful, vain, and ambitious woman who, against Grady's wishes, declined to have children which might have ruined her figure and impeded her social ambitions. She encouraged, guided, and drove her husband in her compulsion to achieve wealth and social recognition. Assisted by Lola in researching her family tree, Sadie discovered she was distantly related to Daniel Boone, and added the name to hers.

Sadie measured everyone in life by what degree they served her power and self image. Lola was an asset to Sadie as long as Will was alive. After Will's death and Lola's descent to less than wealthy, Sadie had less and less use for Lola. Grady wanted children, and hopefully a son, and when I was born he requested I be given his name and he be declared my Godfather. I was named William after my grandfather, Lola's husband, and Grady after my Godfather, H. Grady Meador.

At the time I was born, H. Grady Meador had become president of Gulf Oil Company, a position he held for decades. Sadie 'Boone' Meador allowed Grady's gesture towards Lola's grandson only to humor Grady, with no intention of allowing it to become anything but a gesture. As the knowledge of Katherine's early struggles came to his attention, Grady offered to adopt his namesake, but Sadie went behind his back and told Lola it was not to be.

The year we were in Staten Island, Grady became 'Rex; King of Mardi Gras,' the highest social achievement possible in New Orleans and accorded only multi-multi-millionaires who could afford the immense sums required.

When we returned to New Orleans, I would sometimes accompany Lola on outings with Uncle Grady and Aunt Sadie, sometimes visit their home in Meterie, and sometimes stay with Lola when she would housesit for them during their travels. When at his home, Grady would sometimes take his Rex crown out of its' glass case on the stair landing and let me wear it with a lot of tissue paper stuffed inside to make it fit. It had been made for him in Austria of white gold with amethyst, zircon, and pearl jeweling at a cost of $13,500 which, in today's value, amounts to hundreds of thousands. I remember one time house sitting with Lola while Grady and Sadie were traveling on the Queen Mary. One night Lola received a radio-telephone call from Sadie who was in the middle of the Atlantic and was calling to verify instructions she had given the butler regarding their return. The black full-time butler was a multi-talented and immensely patient man who could tolerate all Sadie's condescending ways and still manage to run the household and its occasional staff with total efficiency. He was also her uniformed chauffeur and would drive her to ten different grocery stores so she could buy all the different sale items, managing to keep a straight face despite the fact that she was spending more to run around than she was saving on sale items.

But when we weren't visiting Lola's affluent friends, life on Patton Street was far more modest and the fare far less than 'haute cuisine.' At this point, Lo had spent a decade learning how to live a little less high on the hog than she had when her husband was alive. Her teachers had not been her affluent friends, but rather the 'little people' who made up the everyday life on Patton Street.

This was a time when there were still street vendors plying their wares. There was the 'rag and bone man,' a black man in a horse drawn cart which announced his presence with its clinking clanking strand of bottles and cans strung above his head as he held the reins of his woebegone horse. He would collect your clean washed bottles, tin cans, rendered bones, and old clothing, offering you a few pennies if you asked, but hoping to accept them as donations if you were generous. There were walking vendors with huge baskets of their particular home grown fruit or vegetable, sometimes carried on their head, hawking their "straaaaaaaaw-berrieeeeees" or "whoa-tahmelooooon" or "alla-gator peaaaaars" (avocados) in melodious sing-song fashion. The one we kids always waited for was the girl on a bicycle with a tinkling strand of sleigh bells announcing her presence moments before the aroma of her homemade salt water taffy reached your nostrils.

The neighborhood grocery, a block away, was Graffinino's. Its fresh fruit and vegetables were displayed in the barrels and wooden boxes they had arrived in, and, for good customers, these wooden containers were available for your utilitarian and craft needs. The wood from those containers made a lot of our furniture and toys. There was an infinite variety of pastas and dried foods displayed in the glass fronted tip-out bins which the heavyset Mrs. Graffinino would scoop a precise amount from as you watched the scale carefully to assure no ones thumb accidentally rested there. Mr. Graffinino operated the adjacent butcher shop, and there you really had to watch the scales.

His brother operated the tavern across the street. And another brother operated the ice house down the block. The Graffinino ice truck covered the neighborhood daily, followed by small children and our large mongrel dog, Mooch, who begged for small chips of ice from the Graffinino boy who chipped the large blocks into smaller ones and hauled them with ice tongs and a leather wrapper into each kitchen and icebox of regular customers.

There was an old throw rug in our dining room, which served as our living room, on which Mooch was allowed to bring his treasure of ice which he would gnaw on like a bone. Mooch was double jointed and, after finishing his ice treat, would sprawl out and take a nap, his limbs spread in awkward directions that made him look like a Mack truck had hit him.

The patriarch of the Graffininos was 'Tony the fruit man' who once or twice a week drove his old truck through the neighborhood with its open sloping sides displaying a variety of fruits and vegetables. Mr. Tony was slightly shorter than Lola, his hair and mustache somewhat whiter than her sparse hair, and he always wore a felt brimmed hat, long sleeved checkered shirts, and a vest.

Many a time I saw Mr. Tony instruct Lola in the delicate art of being poor. Lo would look over the goods, inquire about prices, frown slightly, then start to leave without buying anything. This time Mr. Tony gestured toward her with one hand. "Aye, Mz. Smits, why you no buy no-ting? You no likka my fruits?"

"I can't afford your prices, Mr. Graffinino."

"My prices, she'sa low. You no got lower prices anywhere. That'sa no why you no buy."

"Mr. Graffinino, let's just say I can't afford to buy anything today."

Mr. Tony took his hat off and spoke softly. "Mz. Smits, forgive me, but … ..mebbe you wanna credit. You wanna credit, you gotta credit."

Lo looked down embarrassed. "Thank you, Mr. Graffinino, but I couldn't do that."

"Mz. Smits, whaddeya wan' dis banana for?"

"To make banana bread."

"Mz. Smits, you no need dis banana. She'sa prima vera, perfect golden yellow. She'sa for de table, por la mano, to eat by hand. Whad you need is dis banana. She'sa cost a quarter whad yellow banana cost. She'sa black on de outside, but she'sa fine on de inside. Look!" And he pulled the black peel aside to reveal an unblemished white interior.

Little by little Lo took the well meaning tips to heart. On another occasion Mr. Tony said, "Mz. Smits, Christmas she'sa comma soon. You makka de fruitcake?"

"Possibly, Mr. Graffinino."

"You makka de fruitcake, Mz. Smits, you needa de citron candy."

"Citron candy, Mr. Graffinino?"

"De liddle piece-a fruits you put in de fruitcake, Mz. Smits. Now you ged ready, you buy de lemon, de lime, de orange, all widda nice smooth skin, and you peel de skin like dis, Mz. Smits." He took out his huge pocket knife, what we'd call a switchblade today, and peeled a lemon swiftly and meticulously so the rind was in four intact quarters. These he cut into minute strips. "You do dis wid all fruit widda rind, den you boil de pieces of rind in melted sugar for fifteen, thirdy minutes, mebbe longer. Strain it, dry it under a screen in de sun, you got 'citron candy' for you fruitcake, and good to eat all by itself."

This went on for years. Then one day, Mr. Tony took his hat off as Lola started to leave with her vegetables. "Scuza, Ms. Smits, but, issa true your bertday today?"

Lola smiled. "Why yes, Mr. Graffinino, how did you know."

"You grandchild. I hear her talka you grandson. Mz. Smits, you mind iffa I givva you dis?" And he proffered a bottle of wine.

Lola was flustered, but flattered. "Why, Mr. Graffinino, I don't know what to say."

Mr. Tony smiled charmingly. "Jus say 'yes,' Mz. Smits."

It was a moment of realization for Lola as she took the bottle and looked and spoke to Mr. Tony as she never had before. "Why, thank you, Mr. Graffinino, but I can only accept this if you'll be kind enough to share it with me."

"If you like, Mz. Smits, I be honored." Mr. Tony joined Lola on the front porch as she instructed my sister, Thelma, to open the bottle and serve it on a tray with two wine glasses. When Thelma returned with ice in the glasses, Lo started to chide her about the ice, but Mr. Tony stopped her. "Thassa fine, Mz. Smits. We drinka dis way alla time."

As Thelma poured the wine, Lola attempted small talk, it was "Mr. Graffinino" this and "Mr. Graffinino" that.

Finally, Mr. Tony reached for his glass and said, "Mz. Smits, justa for today, justa dis once, mebbe be okay you calla me, Tony?" He saluted her with his glass. "Justa for today, okay?"

Lo picked up her glass and said, "Of course, Mister … .., of course, Tony. And you must call me Lola."

Mr. Tony shook his head slowly. "Oh no, I could'na do dat." Then he smiled. "But, mebbe be okay I call you Miss Lola?"

Lo smiled back at him. "Whatever you like, Tony."

Mr. Tony raised his glass on high. "To Miss Lola, on her bert-day. May dere be many more."

Lo raised her glass. "To Tony, and his family, and our friendship. Thank you, Tony Graffinino." And their glasses met.

It may not have been a total social revolution, but, in 1940, for Lola Inez Schmidt, it was a milestone.

At this point in her life, Lo was still in the Catholic phase of her search for spiritual peace. She attended St. Patrick's Cathedral on Camp Street a few short blocks from City Hall in downtown New Orleans. The priest at that time was Father Carre, a short balding feisty little Italian man who was a politician, a revolutionary, and a dynamo of good deeds and clandestine sensual living.

Our first exposure to him was through Lo who, unknown to my mother and against her wishes, took me to Father Carre and had me baptized Catholic. Father Carre formerly became my spiritual Godfather and gave me a second middle name, Raymond. I was now William Grady Ramondo Thomas, inheritor of Swiss, German, Welch, Irish, American Indian, and now Italian cultures. Katherine was infuriated that any spiritual preference had been imposed on one of her children, but, as Lo and Father Carre reasoned, "How can it hurt."

Father Carre had an eye for and a way with the

ladies. He pacified Katherine regarding my baptism and talked her into adding her talents as a violinist to the already impressive services at St. Patrick's. The high vaulted cathedral had a gold plated alter, a huge pipe organ that sometimes needed the emergency assistance of fireman from across the street to hand pump the ailing compressor, and an award winning choir that rivaled in size and professionalism any I've ever seen since.

Father Carre's beautiful niece was the lead soprano with the choir, and my brother would attend services just to worship her from afar. Thelma would attend because it was a good excuse to dress up. I would attend to hear Katherine's violin and the fabulous pipe organ in concert. And Lo would attend as the only family member seeking spiritual solace and guidance.

Father Carre was, indeed, a good man. He was also audacious. He had speakers installed in the park in front of City Hall two blocks away so all the bums sleeping there would be exposed to the sermon as well as the beautiful music. He had a little red Ford that he liked to drive too fast and used on his errands of mercy like some comic book hero racing to the rescue.

He had a mistress, a handsome mature blonde lady, who anyone close to him could see barely submerged in the background. And he also had the hots for Katherine, at least, I once saw him chasing her around the furniture, but I don't think he ever caught her.

In any case, St. Patrick's was, musically speaking, one of the most beautiful places of worship among the many in which I heard Katherine play. I cannot hear *Ave Maria* without hearing that magnificent pipe organ and choir.

Father Carre was one of the truly good people who came to our rescue in times of need and gave us some understanding of the options formal religion tries to offer. Father Carre became a Monseigneur and, despite all his daredevil races in his little red Ford, sometimes on his way to our rescue, he died in a collision while in the back seat of a limousine being backed out of St. Patrick's driveway by his loving nephew.

Two blocks from the apartment house on Patton was another Catholic institution that gave me a confusing glimpse of the clergy, a cloistered nunnery covering an entire huge city block and surrounded by a twelve foot high brick fence. A huge oak tree grew in the middle of one side street bordering it and, as I learned from the neighborhood boys, climbing up and sitting in the crotch of the tree gave one a bird's eye view of the mysterious goings on inside. I watched these silent pensive looking ladies go about their daily chores, respond to vesper bells like Pavlov's dogs, and sometimes kneel on the second floor balcony and awkwardly flog their own backs with small knotted whips while mouthing soundless entreaties to some concept of God I could not share with them.

I wondered about Aunt Thelma's abortive attempt to become a nun and wondered if she fared any better with Bob Morris.

Because of the proximity to Audubon Park, this neighborhood was considered an appropriately quiet retreat for such institutions. Five blocks away was St. Vincent dePaul's Sanitarium, the state operated insane asylum which we'd pass while promenading on Exposition Boulevard, always hoping we'd see some deviant behavior in the patients who wandered the yards peacefully and never fulfilled our imagined expectations.

Much more entertaining and enlightening was the Home For Incurables which occupied the entire city block next to ours and was adjacent to the nunnery. The beautiful old colonnaded brick plantation style two story curved building was surrounded by park-like grounds with curved walkways and mature oak trees. It was a repository for what were considered 'hopeless' cases in that day; paraplegics, epileptics, and cases of polio, advanced rhombuses, crippling arthritis, gross deformities, or whatever was incurable and didn't fall under the aegis of other institutions.

At the staff's request, Katherine volunteered her services as a masseuse and primarily worked with the young male paraplegics who would have wheelchair races in the hallways and vie to see who would have me as their passenger in the race, probably because I would squeal with delight and be ecstatic if we won. I remember a young man named Delbert who happily picked me up and plopped me in his lap, only to wince with pain and angrily ask what I had in my pocket, whereupon I innocently produced a can of sardines from my back pocket and explained, "Them's little fishes, I cuts their tails off and eats 'em," much to the amusement of all around.

There was the old man with rhombuses who would move as if in slow motion along the curved walkways, sit for hours on the concrete benches, and feed the many squirrels and pigeons who would clamber all over him as if he were a statue. I would sit beside him and he would teach me to remain perfectly still, then move with slow Shiatsu grace that would reassure the squirrels enough to climb upon my knee and pigeons to light upon my arm and eat out of my hand.

There was Sherman, a man who had been a 'blue baby' and expected to die in infancy, but who survived and was then in his thirties, still slightly blue in complexion at times, and educated as a very competent electrician. One characteristic of his unique physiological makeup allowed him to handle live electric wires with no pain nor consequences to his body. In subsequent years, Sherman was kind enough to rewire one of the Bay houses for us.

There were people with twisted bodies and sad eyes who peered from darkened rooms where they were hidden from the world. There were people who were human vegetables that were taken out for strolls in their hospital gowns in order to air their bodies and change their bed linens. And there was at least one lady who should have been at dePaul's Sanatarium because she would periodically go berserk, tear all her clothes off, and start accosting men in the hallways. Sometimes she succeeded in escaping the grounds and gave the whole neighborhood a thrill.

The Pardees, an elderly couple who had purchased the corner house from Lola, hardly ever left their house. A.J. used to play chess with the old man, and I would be admonished to stay out of their way as the old lady would complain of my youthful noisiness. They passed away while we were living there, and the house was purchased by a couple from down the block who had an only son about a year older than I.

Jackie had what I considered a warped outlook on the world. He used to delight in teaching me bad words and watching me suffer the results at Lo's hands. Usually Lo just washed my mouth out with the foul tasting Octagon soap, an eight-sided brown bar of highly caustic soap most people reserved for laundry use. Once my mother was home when Lo attempted to snip the end of my tongue with scissors to cure me of bad language, and Katherine's defiance of Lo's old fashioned disciplinary measures brought about a more amicable relationship between me and my grandmother.

Jackie's folks were related to John Churchill Chase, the internationally famous political cartoonist with the New Orleans Item. Chase used to send personally illustrated letters and postcards to some of his relatives, much like Katherine and Aunt Thelma's father had sent them when they were away at school, but Jackie's parents did not appreciate them as art and threw them in the trash where we'd retrieve them. After meeting Chase through them, Chase was flattered by our family's admiration and would give us the original artwork of many of his cartoons that we praised. Some of these were framed on our walls along with the work of other artists we knew and admired.

Jackie's family was Catholic and his development in later years seemed arrested in early adolescence. He never had normal relationships with his peers and, at an early age and much to his mother's delight, he entered the priesthood. In his midlife he committed suicide.

But, back when he was the only boy my age on the block, his parents enclosed the understructure of the corner house to create two rental apartments. Their first tenants were two sisters close to Katherine's age, Mary and Edna Isom. Edna was taller, blonde, and a nurse by profession. Mary was short, brunette, and a medical artist by profession, and our family fell in love with her in varying degrees. She was very attractive, very talented, and a little eccentric; in other words, our kind of people.

Katherine admired Mary's artistic talents, which were considerable in her field and shared by her brother, John, who was a successful commercial artist with one of the nation's leading advertising agencies in New York City. Katherine was enthralled with John's airbrush painting of a Four Roses Whiskey magazine ad which was the first of his work we saw in Mary's apartment. A.J. and I admired Mary as a very attractive woman, but A.J., who was almost sixteen at the time, was the only one mature enough to understand the attraction we felt. Our association with Mary Isom accelerated our artistic interests which Katherine had founded with craft projects. Mary was experimenting with small sculptures at the time, and plaster casts and reproductions from them. This led us to experiment with casting techniques and papier mache sculptures, which in turn found expression in creating marionette dolls.

Part of this turn of events was prompted by Katherine's newfound job with the WPA, President

Roosevelt's Work Projects Administration, which was one of various efforts to create employment during the depression. For the magnificent sum of $25 a month, Katherine traveled through the rural countryside teaching crafts, folk music, and various homemaking skills to the housewives and homemakers who were mostly uneducated and often illiterate. She taught such practical and cultural things as how to make candle holders and kerosene lamp reflectors from tin cans, how to make children's dolls from clothespins and bottles, and how to sing French and Indian and Anglo folk songs to families whose economics afforded them no other entertainment options.

Marionette shows were one of these skills Katherine brought back and compounded with Mary Isom's talents until we children had our own full fledged marionette show, replete with portable proscenium made from old drapes suspended on poles supported by standing lamp bases. The opening was made from the surviving three sides of an elaborate gilded gesso picture frame, and the satin curtains salvaged from an old dress and activated by curtain drawstrings just like the most professional of stages.

The marionettes mostly started from the basis of a salvaged doll head and bodies we would design, build, and costume ourselves. Thelma had an elaborately dressed Spanish lady marionette named Conchita. A.J. had a clown named Happy, a knight in armor given various names from English history which he had studied with his private tutor in Canada, and a very clever skeleton doll named Archibald. I, on the other hand, had a penchant for non-human dolls.

The first was prompted by a visit to a Japanese novelty shop on Royal Street in the French Quarter. Mr. Hanada's tiny little shop was full of the mysteries of the orient, plus the tantalizing aroma of fresh rice cakes cooked on a griddle in the front window of the shop by his pretty daughter. Mr. Hanada was close to Lo's age and shared a warm cultural acquaintanceship with her, which led her to grieve for his hardships and internment during the war years.

Among the many items I admired and acquired from his shop, was a fist-sized gesso cast elaborately painted dragon's head whose lower jaw, eyes, and ears animated via strings attached to a bent bamboo spring at the rear of the head. Possibly it was intended for use as a hand puppet, which is the use I put it to with the help of Katherine who stitched up a wine velvet sleeve with a gilded gauze back fin and black and gold hand-painted scales. Putting the puppet on like a sleeve, manipulating the bamboo spring to articulate its face, and blowing cigarette smoke through a rubber tube that ran down to his mouth, 'Clarence The Dragon' became an instant hit. We wrote our own plays and, when my first attempt to blow cigarette smoke out his mouth caused me to cough, the resulting audience laugh prompted me to keep the cough in the script with the added line, "I have to smoke, being a fire-eating dragon and all, but you'd think humans who don't have to would know better."

The hand puppet was easier for me, being the youngest, to manipulate. But, as my skills increased, the next character in my repertoire was a black velvet spider with silver glittered markings and eight legs made by winding wire on a pencil to make long springs which terminated in feet made from lead fishing sinkers. This 'string puppet,' or marionette, had no dialogue, but instead tap danced on a sheet of glass with musical synchronization, if not Fred Astaire perfection. 'Taps The Spider' and 'Clarence The Dragon' were often comical antagonists to A.J.'s knights in armor, or even 'Archibald The Skeleton' who was often a sword wielding hero of sorts.

My final star of marionette fame was 'Pete The Penguin,' made from a peanut butter jar with a black velvet and white satin skin, a large conical plastic bead for a beak, two gummed page hole reinforcers for eyes, and two fabric encased nickels stitched on as floppy feet. Pete did not have to be an antagonist in the dynamic scheme of our little theater company, and he was a natural to give rein to my desire to write satirical comedy. He was sarcastic, he was audacious, and he dared to do many of the things the youngest of three children might have been too inhibited to do.

Our little marionette theater was more than successful on Patton Street, it was invited by Father Carre and others to do guest benefit performances at the Home For Incurables, St. Patrick's Cathedral, and a number of other hosts around town who actually raised money for charities with our show, even though we had to carry our equipment on foot for many blocks at times for want of carfare to our engagement. We never asked for a cent to perform, being flattered to be invited to perform, and being thrilled by the positive audience response we always received.

However, I do remember once when we were doing our usual 'after the show routine' of taking the dolls out front and showing people how they worked. Often people would want to tease Clarence to see if he would bite them, and I would oblige by nipping at their fingers with his red, black, and gold painted jaws. Father Carre came over to me and pretended to be fearful of proffering his finger to be bitten by Clarence. As I clamped Clarence's jaws over Father Carre's pudgy fingers, I felt something fall into my hand. Father Carre winked at me and walked away as I stared down Clarence's throat to find a fifty cent piece in my hand, marking my first professional appearance in show business.

(left to right) Thelma, A.J., the author at age 5, and Mary Isom holding Schnapsie, demonstrating their marionettes.

Bottom left: Book Cover designed and executed by Mary Isom.
Bottom right: *(left to right)* Delbert, the author aged 4, Thelma, Sherman, and Henry at The Home For Incurables.

Above: a John Churchill Chase cartoon in the *New Orleans Item* celebrates the 1930 opening of the Municipal Auditorium which hosts cultural performances and many of the Mari Gras balls, including those of Comus and Rex Krewes on Mardi Gras night.

Above: H. Grady Meador, President of Gulf Oil for many years, 1939 Rex King of Mardi Gras, and godfather to the author who was given the middle name 'Grady' to signify that relationship.

Chapter Six
CHECKERBOARD

To my knowledge, New Orleans had no black ghettos during the 1930's and 40's of my youth. After World War II, the well meaning civic administrations did what all major cities did, they built low income housing called 'projects' which immediately became ghettos that changed the face of the city for the worse for years to come. But, in my youth, New Orleans was a 'checkerboard' city, as were many in the South. There would be a block of white housing, then a block of black, then a half and half block, and so on.

There was an integration of sorts that probably stemmed from the fact that blacks existed in the city, even in the days of slavery, in the capacity of domestics, artisans, mechanics, and all the services that were an integral part of the white residential needs. Unlike plantations or factories where the labor force and product could be dislocated from the white population, a city that does not deny the talents of all its citizens must distribute those talents more or less evenly across the face of the city. The best butcher or baker or candlestick maker are not going to be located according to their complexion, but rather where the best products or services are most appreciated and most rewarded.

The earliest blacks to reside in New Orleans were often 'freedmen,' individuals whose exceptional talents led them to be freed from slavery as a reward from a grateful or admiring owner. By the time of emancipation, many of these freedmen were deeply entrenched in the commerce of New Orleans and other major southern cities as artisans, tradesmen, and landowners. Despite the social and legal segregation, which doubtless took its toll on the psyche of black children born and raised in it, there was a cultural and professional integration which served the best interests of all the colors of New Orleans ethnic stew.

Before the age of 'thinking big,' mass media merchandising, and computerized personnel departments, an individual's talents and abilities were proven only by the reality of their products and performance. Exceptional blacks benefitted from New Orleans tendency, as an internationally flavored city, to recognize and reward quality wherever and in whoever it was to be found. But, that was before New Orleans and the economy in general became too big for its britches and fell into the hands of 'big business.'

Big business doesn't make two dozen fresh apple pies a day for a small neighborhood in a family bakery where the owner built the one brick oven with his own hands. Big business makes two hundred thousand pies a day with enough preservative in them to allow them to sit on the shelf a month, if necessary. And if it's a black creation such as sweet potato pie or an Italian creation such as pizza pie, big business just prints the appropriate ethnic image on the label and in the advertising.

The problem is not that big business makes something that's not as fresh, that's loaded with questionable chemicals, or that's misrepresented as 'original' when in fact it was probably made by Vietnamese immigrants in New Jersey. The problem is that the guy who used to make it no longer can participate in free enterprise, no longer has pride in what he does or hope for the future, and has to move to New Jersey to work for the competitive wages of a Vietnamese immigrant.

Now, a given house or block of New Orleans real estate does not remain in one family for generations to be given by the family patriarch or matriarch to their descendants; male or female, legitimate or illegitimate, white or black. Now, capital does not concentrate in the hands of individuals who invest it at their own discretion in small businesses whose products or services the investor knows by personal experience to be superior. Now, champions and crusaders are not individuals who respond to an inequity with the risk of their own personal capital and the sweat of their own two hands.

Today, land is the province of 'developers' who are not individuals with an individual sense of right or wrong or fairness or worthiness. Developers are conglomerates who exercise massive economic and political pressure to change the face of huge sections of any city based primarily, despite any altruistic claims by their vice president in charge of public relations, on the profit motive.

The patriarch or matriarch of the family sees their descendants disperse in an age of mobility, and they sell their land to the developers. The individual with capital sees a safer alternative than making personal loans to worthy families for small businesses, so he invests it through financial institutions who lend it to the developers. And the champions and crusaders hire the same Madison Avenue media specialists who contributed to the problem to help them complain about the problem and seek somebody else's money to correct it.

The scale of the checkerboard has changed from a fine evenly distributed collection of black and white families and businesses who knew each other and did not fear each other because they rubbed elbows together in their daily life. It changed into a gross uneven pattern divided into huge subdivisions of 'upwardly mobile' whites surrounding huge black ghettos looming like a cancer in the inner city. New Orleans can take little solace in smugly arguing that this process took place in northern cities a hundred years ago. The progress of big business and bureaucracy has brought the illness to this beautiful one of a kind city, and, as it looks to America's other great cities formerly and similarly afflicted, there is no cure in sight.

But there was a time, back at the beginning of the 1940's in New Orleans, when Lola's black maid, Ethyl, lived only a few blocks from Patton Street, persevered with Lola's frequent inability to pay her part time wages on time, and regarded Lo and her children with tolerance, affection, and a sense of 'family.'

Ethyl was a sturdily built lady, probably in her thirties then, dark and passably attractive in an Africanze way. She was a physically and emotionally strong woman. Her placid unsmiling face was her protection when dealing with two or more whites in the everyday life of cleaning house, doing laundry, or preparing food. Her ferocious frown could intimidate any child into behaving. And her rare moments of expressiveness were reserved for the privacy of dealing with one family member at a time. Then she could laugh or cry, advise or implore, and drop the mask she carried around most of the time.

Ethyl was fiercely protective of Lola. She had seen Lola's assets stripped from her by family and friends, her naivete taken advantage of by local tradesmen, and knew that some of her former maids had unkindly stolen some of the sterling flatware and even some of her few remaining jewels. At rare private moments, which I was unwittingly privy to behind my screened off corner of the kitchen, Ethyl would chide Lola for allowing herself to be victimized, encourage her to be assertive, and sometimes hold her in her arms when Lola cried.

Ethyl probably thought of the presence of Katherine and her children as yet another unkind burden upon Lola. Certainly we children were the focus of a lot of her complaints about the added work we created, and, living in the kitchen and being young enough to still get into a lot of dirt, I came in for more than my share of the complaints.

Just as I grudgingly came to respect Lo as a woman who had done the best she could with setbacks in life and was valiantly trying to step into the enlightened first half of the 20th century, I grudgingly came to respect Ethyl as a woman whose gruff exterior was a reasonable defense against injustices which she was aware of, but did not know fully how to deal with.

Behind the apartment house were some sheds whose exterior walls were made entirely of green wooden louvered shutters which I suspect once adorned the windows of some defunct house. The sheds contained storage, laundry tubs, and something I heretofore never knew existed. While playing in the shed, inventorying how many partially used cans of paint and shellac were available for future craft projects, I would see Ethyl enter a door at the end of the shed, remain for five or ten minutes, and exit to the sound of a flushing toilet. When I queried her why she went to the trouble to come out here to use a toilet, she answered in a resentful tone, "This is the maid's toilet." When I asked, with the innocence of a babe out of whose mouth wisdom rarely came, why there should be such a thing as a 'maid's toilet,' she answered in the same tone, "Ask yo' granma," and slammed the green shuttered door.

Lo's answer to the effect that "it has always been so" simply prompted the inevitable "why has it always been so?"

Lo's complaint "you ask too many questions" was my signal to cease and desist, unless I wanted my mouth washed out with Octagon soap. But I think I prompted Lo to ask herself those questions, because she was very pensive the rest of that afternoon. I can't remember how long after that it was, maybe months, maybe a year, but I recall a day when Lo invited Ethyl to use the inside bathroom and the 'maid's toilet' was devoted to the ever increasing need for storage space.

In subsequent years, however, there were times when Lo was the crusader and Ethyl the traditionalist fighting against her own best interests. Mr. Chatters was a middle aged black postman whose good manners and fine English led Lola to engage him in conversation. She learned that he had put all his children into college. One was a doctor, another a university professor. The youngest was in a local black college majoring in music and currently performing in her initial recital. Lo wanted to attend the performance and Mr. Chatters promised to bring tickets the next day.

He arrived with the tickets in the hottest part of the day and Lola, anticipating his arrival and appreciative of the heat, invited him into the living room for lemonade and instructed Ethyl to serve it. He hesitantly accepted the seat Lola ushered him to, but, when Ethyl arrived with the lemonade and glared at him, he got up and stood by his seat to drink his lemonade, tactfully dismissing Lola's entreaties for him to resume his seat.

After he left, Ethyl was infuriated and scolded Lola for compromising her reputation by inviting him in, transgressing the unwritten code by asking him to be seated as an equal in her home, and embarrassing Ethyl by asking her as a domestic to serve another black person. No amount of reasoning could change her attitude. Now it was Ethyl's turn to ponder the illogic of tradition. I don't know if she ever made a similar transition such as Lo had about the bathroom, and, if so, I don't know if she made that transition in more or less time than it had taken Lo. I do know Lo attended the recital and, in subsequent performances at Xavier University and other black performance venues over the following years, so did Katherine and we children.

When we visited the old Hamburg homestead outside of Natchez, we met another black regarded as family. Jesse James was the son of the one and only family slave. I often thought how different we were from most other 'genteel' southern families who boasted of 'Colonels' in the Confederate Army or of plantations filled with slaves, or conversely, their family's history unblemished with slaveholding. We had only one family member in the Confederate Army, a lowly enlisted man, and we were tainted with being a slaveholder, one single slave who, it was said, was treated far better than his owners children or mules as he was far more productive and valuable.

But Jesse James regarded us without malice and, as we did him, as 'family.' Jesse was mature, even back then, and lived to a ripe old age, but nobody, including Jesse, knew for a fact what that age was.

He was a dark, handsome, and well built man who compensated for a lack of vocabulary and literacy with a wealth of woodsy folklore and knowledge of nature. He could tell north without a compass (moss grows on the north side of the tree), the approximate temperature without a thermometer (he counted cricket chirps), and the projected weather for the next few days based on a series of natural signs I never fully understood. Most of his conversation consisted of the response, "Thassright," which did not prevent him from being a deacon in his church and occasionally preaching the gospel which he had committed to memory without being able to read one word of the 'good book.'

Jesse's wife, Lula Mae, was very fair, bore an uncanny resemblance to Lola, and was most probably Lola's half sister by virtue of her father's, Charles Magee's, wild oats. Lula Mae was as gentle and lovable as Lo, was literate, and had been Jesse's tutor in memorizing the gospel. The two of them had always lived on the homestead, and, before it was sold off in later years, the family gave Jesse and Lula Mae the five acres on which their house was built.

The Schmidts supported Xavier University, St. Augustine's Seminary, and the cultural pursuits of Lo's mailman, Mr. Chatters, children with program ads, donations, and personal attendance by Lo's family, children, and grandchildren

Like New Orleans, Bay St. Louis was also checkerboarded. In fact, every southern city or town I was in prior to the postwar period was checkerboarded. Bay St. Louis had a smaller black population than most southern towns, probably because it was primarily a beach resort area with no degree of farming or industry to support a working class population. Being seasonally populated with gentry from New Orleans also made it a more liberal environment than most small southern towns.

From the time of the Civil War there had been a black parochial school, St. Rose deLima. After the turn of the century, there had been America's first black seminary, St. Augustines. When we first arrived in the Bay and I was born, the family on the opposite corner, the Rochains, were black. To be more accurate, they were 'high yeller,' they were very well mannered, and they were very standoffish about playing with us until it could be verified that we didn't have head lice. The white family who lived behind us had numerous blonde haired bullying lice ridden children who had infected everyone in the neighborhood except the Rochains.

A little more than a block behind us lived the Pienas family, a black family originally from Puerto Rico. Mrs. Pienas looked like a caricature of a black mammy and fulfilled many aspects of a Caribbean stereotype from tropical cuisine right down to believing in and practicing voodoo. When she would sometimes babysit us, she would scare the hell out of us on foggy nights by making us all huddle in the middle hallway while she thumb tacked newspaper to the windows to "keep out the evil spirits."

As an occasional domestic, she was privy to a lot of classified information. She probably knew almost as much about the skeletons in the town closets as Dr. Horton did, but, in Mrs. Pienas, it was filtered through a very superstitious mind. I remember one day when we were in the living room and Mrs. Pienas spied two young white men walking down the street. She pulled me over to the window, pointed at them, and said, "Never never go near those young men. They be very very evil. Evil and degenerate."

When Katherine came home, I asked her what 'degenerate' meant. When she wanted to know why, I told her about the two young men. It wasn't until I was almost grown that she explained what Mrs. Pienas was upset about.

It seems the two young men were longtime house guests of Mrs. Moreau, the ageing and wealthy lady who lived around the corner on Carrol Avenue at the beach. Mrs. Moreau had inherited a small fortune from her deceased husband. She was in the habit of bringing home young men from New Orleans and these two were her most recently acquired 'companions.' One of them was Tennessee Williams, and the other William's lifetime companion.

Mrs. Moreau also knew a lot about the skeleton's in the town closets, and she obviously shared more of the town's secrets with Williams than the townsfolk appreciated. Tennessee Williams wrote most of his famous works about the scandals of the people of Bay St. Louis. Many years later, one of his least known works, *This House Is Condemned*, was made into a movie and filmed in Bay St. Louis. Robert Redford and Natalie Wood played the lead characters who actually lived in the Bay in the very house used as the locale. I worked briefly in a menial capacity on the film,

Mrs. Pienas teenage daughter, Rosalie, was a very beautiful and lovable girl, and the whole family fell in love with her, A.J. the hardest. One of our profound regrets at being poor was that we could not have Rosalie with us all the time.

At the end of the block behind us was a black man named Ogeese Saucier who had two sons close to my age, also some chickens, ducks, and goats. The two boys, the older one closest to my age was Tony, would hitch the older nanny goat to a cart and make the rounds of the neighborhood to collect the 'slop' (edible waste) most families would save for them. I played with Tony and his brother, helped feed the chickens and ducks, and would sometimes be rewarded by being allowed to ride on the goat cart when they collected slop. Our friendship continued up until the time we left for Staten Island.

Upon our eventual return to the Bay, I expressed a desire to renew my friendship with them, but was told that was inappropriate. Again, the answers to my questions were unsatisfactory; that we attended two different schools, that we were supposed to grow into two different societies, and that was "just the way it was." I felt a painful sense of loss at not being able to enjoy Tony's smile, at not having a little brother like Tony's little brother, and at not being able to ride on the goat cart anymore.

Even so, Bay St. Louis and New Orleans were more racially liberated than other southern towns and cities where segregation was more noticeable and economic opportunity more polarized. Still, the South in general was better in these regards than some other parts of the United States I experienced living in. Even such grass roots as the black children I knew in school on Staten Island, while they may not have been legally segregated, were socially and emotionally divorced from the white population with a crippling bitterness that was never manifested in my childhood or adult relations with Southern blacks.

The black social worker on Staten Island who hassled my mother about my ambidexterity in school had been born and raised in New York, and she was prepared to do battle with the poor white family from Mississippi whom she automatically assumed were going to be militant bigots. She was militantly defensive to the point of being rude and belligerent, only to find, to her confusion, that there was no bigotry to defend herself against. Ultimately, she apologized to Katherine for her assumptions and became an amiable friend.

Unfortunately, there is no place on this earth totally devoid of bigotry, and Bay St. Louis had its small but shameful share. There was an incident I recall during the war years involving a butcher who shot a black man dead in the rear of the butcher shop during business hours. The inquest declared it self defense, but too many people, both black and white, felt the circumstances were questionable enough to have warranted a trial. I was just a child, did not witness the incident, and was not present at the inquest, but, in my heart and based on the integrity of the people who questioned the verdict of the inquest, I fear there was a racially motivated miscarriage of justice and a stain upon the otherwise liberal and wholesome environment of the Bay.

There was another incident which I was witness to as I was integrally involved. It revolved around another neighbor, an elderly black man who lived across the street from Ogeese and his two sons at the end of the block behind us. Probably in his sixties at the time, he looked like Uncle Remus with his dark skin, white hair and full beard, and the denim overalls which were his usual attire. There was a shed beside his house which housed a mountain of old clothes, because he was a 'rag picker' who collected folks unwanted clothing in a homemade handcart and sold the best of the used clothing to those of us too poor to shop retail. Periodically a truck would come and pick up the worst of the pile as rag salvage for the paper mills.

I suppose we wore more than a few garments purchased from that huge pile he was endlessly sorting through. But the item I specifically remember purchasing was the tattered remnant of a red velvet dress from which Katherine made me a cape for a king's costume she was making for me.

I, and my family, were devotee's of the *Prince Valiant* comic strip which depicted in beautiful artwork and well researched authenticity the adventures of the English knights of old. A.J. had made me a wooden sword which Katherine jeweled to simulate Prince Valiant's 'singing sword.' I had made myself a jeweled crown, collar, and belt from cardboard and old broken pieces of costume jewelry. And this beautiful Mandarin red velvet dress I spied in the rag picker's pile was to be the final touch to the ensemble. I bargained with him and ended up getting the tattered piece for fifty cents.

There came a time in the mid 1940's when the old man's daughter came to stay with him in the final stages of her pregnancy. This was a time when the Bay had grown in population and there were several new younger doctors to take up the slack that Dr. Horton could not fulfill alone. One of the more successful and pompous was a handsome man around forty with a spiffy vanDyke and goatee. He lived around the corner from us on Carrol Avenue near the beach, almost directly across from Mrs. Moreau's house.

One night we heard a woman's screams coming from the old man's house and I was sent to inquire if they needed help. I remember my fear as I approached the house, hearing the screams grow louder and seeing a frantically moving shadow against the window curtains lighted by kerosene lamps. I wondered if violence was afoot and someone was being murdered.

As I knocked on the door with its acid etched patterned glass panel, the old man snatched the door open so abruptly I jumped back, startled. His face was wide eyed and tears were streaming down his cheeks into his white beard. When I timidly asked if they needed help, he grabbed me by the shoulders and said, "Oh, thank God you come, son! Go and fetch a doctor, as quick as you can!"

"Which doctor?"

He shook me by the shoulders. "Any doctor, boy, any doctor! And tell him my girl's havin' a baby, and somethin's terrible wrong!"

"Yessir, I'll fetch Dr. Horton."

"Good boy. Now hurry!" and he almost pushed me off the porch before entering and slamming the door so hard the patterned glass rattled just short of breaking.

I ran to tell Katherine and, together, we dashed across the street to use a neighbor's phone, but Dr. Horton was out on a country call which was likely to be all night. The neighbor suggested the new doctor around the corner, but their phone line was busy, so I was sent to fetch him on foot.

I arrived at his home breathless and grateful to see lights on inside. The lady of the house answered my frantic knocks and was reluctant to call the doctor until I repeated the urgency of the situation several times. The doctor came to the door in pants, stocking feet, and an athletic tee shirt. He listened to my explanation with an impatient frown on his face, then made me repeat the old man's name and address until he was reassured I was talking about a black family.

I remember thinking how handsome and distinguished he looked with his meticulously styled vanDyke and goatee. And I remember how pompous and malicious his words sounded as he said, "I've had a long hard day, those people are not my patients, and I don't do business in that part of town."

I thought to myself, "What part of town? It's around the corner, two blocks from you, in the block I live in." I honestly didn't understand what he was talking about. I tried to hold the door open as he retreated and I said out loud, "But she's in trouble, mother says she's probably having 'complications.'"

The doctor retreated behind the door, stuck his head around it and said, with a painful imitation of a smile, "Listen, son, those niggers drop babies like a bitch drops a litter. She'll do just fine," and he slammed the door in my face.

I ran home in panic and disbelief. I told Katherine what he said and not until I saw the expression on her face and heard the comments she exchanged with the neighbor lady did I finally realize that the doctor had refused assistance because the patient was poor or black or both. Katherine told me to tell the old man I couldn't find anyone, but that she would stay on the phone in hopes of getting Dr. Horton.

With hate in my heart for the new doctor on Carrol Avenue and with tears in my eyes and a heavy sense of guilt for lying, I told the old man that "no one was available."

He leaned heavily on the porch railing as he looked down at me and matched my tears with his own. We could hear his daughter moaning inside the house, too weak to scream anymore. He looked down at the ground, then sniffled as he looked up at the night sky and said, "Yeah, I know. No one's ever available."

I reminded him we'd keep trying to reach Dr. Horton, and he gave me a pained smile. "You do dat. You let me know if you reach him. And, son, you did good." He went inside and shut the door very gently. The next morning Ogeese told us that the old man's daughter had died.

I cannot blame Bay St. Louis for that doctor's behavior, nor even the South, as he was not born nor raised nor educated in the South. I do to some degree blame the AMA and medical schools everywhere for producing an increasingly greed oriented patient insensitive breed of practitioners. I wish I could find some other more specific entity to blame, because the pain and anger I felt that night wells up within me each time I remember the incident and each time I see a similar one in subsequent years, whether the object of the bigotry is the patient's race, creed, economics, or gender.

I cannot fault Bay St. Louis, nor could any of the civil rights groups of the 1950's and 60's. CORE, COFO, and others would arrive in town in a safari of hippie painted vans with leaflets and brochures and media contacts which would lose all interest when no noticeable measure of bigotry and discontent could be found.

One media evaluation of an attempted demonstration was capsulized as, "Bay St. Louis Sat Out The Sit In." The imported civil rights group staged the sit-in at the municipal swimming pier, the totally disinterested local blacks and whites failed to show entirely, and the media could not find one black or white demonstrator who wasn't from out of state, much less out of town.

I was involved in civil rights activities on the West Coast at the time, and it is true that many of the organizations and individuals involved in the rhetoric of that day did a disservice to the valid issues of the movement by looking for conflicts in all the wrong places.

Bay St. Louis did not grow up in the same time nor at the same pace as the most enlightened communities in the world, but it did mature faster and more graciously than most. In Katherine's later years, she became the town librarian. She put her crafts to work making posters, displays, and dioramas to lure children and adults alike to expand their awareness of the world around them through reading.

Despite the fact that she had awkwardly tried to explain to me why I should stop playing with Ogeese's two boys two decades earlier, she quietly went about a scheme to integrate the public library by inviting the black students of St. Rose deLima to attend a weekly lecture she gave, then increased the lectures to two a week, and gradually accustomed the white population to the appearance and participation of blacks in the public library.

Katherine was also quietly instrumental in the town's decision to recognize internationally famous black sculptor Richmond Barthe as the city's most illustrious citizen, Barthe having been born and raised in Bay St. Louis, coincidentally born the same year as my mother. Of course, as luck would have it, the student democratically chosen, by virtue of his top academic scores, to portray Barthe in the centennial pageant just happened to be white, so he appeared in black face. Whoever said that politicians and public relations people have it easy?

To the best of my knowledge, Bay St. Louis is still checkerboard, even if New Orleans has grown cancerous ghettos. To me, the concept of checkerboarding is a possible deterrent to ghetto-izing, and possibly a deterrent to a lot of the other fears and misunderstandings that separation can breed. How to cure the victims in all black ghettos and all white subdivisions of their respective bigotries is like asking how to cure a population of drug addicts, and there seems to be no easy or clear cut answers.

One thing I think most people can agree on, though, and that is, that with drugs or prejudice, the best of all deterrents is open honest education at the earliest possible age. I can think of no better environment for an honest awareness of each other than to live side by side, like the squares of a checkerboard, on a very fine scale, preferably one to one.

The Schmidts supported Xavier University, St. Augustine's Seminary, and the cultural pursuits of Lo's mailman, Mr. Chatters, children with program ads, donations, and personal attendance by Lo's family, children, and grandchildren

Left: Jesse James, the son of the Kinneson family's one and only slave, and Lula Mae, half sister to Lola Schmidt by virtue of Charles Magee's wild oats.

Right, world famous sculptor Richmond Barthe presents a bust of Thelma Thomas to her mother, Katherine Thomas Wilson, for display in the Bay St. Louis Library where Katherine was Head Librarian. Katherine was instrumental in having the City honor Barthe as their most celebrated citizen during their Centennial Celebration in which he was given the Key to the City and represented in a Pageant.

Chapter Seven
MY EARLY BUSINESS CAREER

Our transitional period in New Orleans before returning to Bay St. Louis was a choppy one. Katherine's traveling job with the WPA made it difficult for her to care for three children, particularly the smallest, even after one of the Bay cottages became untenanted and available. So I spent more time with Lo in New Orleans than A.J. and Thelma, who joined Katherine in the Bay within a year after our return from Staten Island.

Eventually, Katherine's schedule allowed me to join them in the second cottage from the corner. This one still didn't have electricity, although the still tenanted corner house, which we had formerly occupied, had been 'electrified' during our absence. Where before the cottages only rented for the summer months to vacationers who considered kerosene lamps and stoves 'quaint,' now the improvement of electric lights attracted a permanent local family who would keep us from our former residence for another year. Now we really felt poor when even our tenants lived better than we did.

After the luxuries of Aunt Thelma's Staten Island house and Lo's New Orleans apartment house, we re-acclimated ourselves to kerosene lamps, kerosene stoves, and wood burning fireplaces. We also re-acclimated ourselves to a very meager income and standard of living. Brown flour gravy and creamed fish on toast re-entered our diet.

We re-entered the local school, a two story brick building one block from our house. Because I was the last to return to the Bay, the school system wanted to set me back. Katherine fought the school authorities all over again, finally making them send a man down from Jackson, the state capital, to interview and test me. As a result, I was bumped ahead a grade instead of back a grade, the first of two times I'd skip a grade in elementary school.

At eight, I was bored with school. I disturbed teachers because I'd finish my work before the others, sneak out of the room, and go listen at the door of the advanced classes. Better teachers would let me sit in the back of the advanced classes. Lesser teachers would get very frustrated trying to regiment me, and I would simply stay at home and only show up for tests which I would barely pass without having cracked a book.

In those days, Mississippi vied with North Dakota to see which would be at the very bottom of the nation's list of educational standards. The school's academic standards were pathetic and, in ten years of attendance, I learned more from two or three good teachers than from the two or three dozen others I frustrated.

At eight I was also bored with poverty. I didn't mind the kerosene lamps, the hand-me-down clothes, or the cold winters so much. It was the wrinkles in my stomach lining that bugged me. Just like I used to hang around the doors to the advanced classes, I started to hang around places that had food in them.

The school bordered on Highway 90, and between the school and the beach, where Highway 90 crossed the wooden bridge across the bay to Henderson Point, there was an antique store owned by Mr. and Mrs. Kenny. This white, wood frame, 'colonial baroque' structure was surrounded by mature oak trees and, in the formally landscaped front yard, a candy stand where a teenage black boy sold 'pralines,' a homemade confection of caramelized sugar and pecans which Mrs. Kenny, aided by several black girls, made in the rear kitchen of the antique store.

I developed a habit of passing by the place when the candy was in the process of being made and all kinds of delicious fragrances wafted out to Highway 90. I would watch the young black vendor, Junior Williams, with the candy basket on one arm as he waved with the other and sang out his wares to the tourist cars that passed. "Peeee-kons, prah-liiiiiines, divinity fuuuuudge!" Cars would pull to the curb and he would dash back and forth to the stand and deliver red net sacks of whole pecans, cellophane bags of shelled pecans, cellophane wrapped pecan logs (strands of fudge rolled in shelled pecans), caramel or chocolate or coconut pralines in wafer thin irregularly shaped three inch discs individually wrapped in waxed paper or a dozen in a box that simulated a miniature bale of cotton, and boxed divinity fudge (a white pecan fudge that literally melts in your mouth).

Sometimes Junior would ask me to fetch him a five cent soft drink from the gas station further down the block, and he'd treat me to one for my trouble. Then Junior took up smoking, but Mrs. Kenny would not let him smoke at the candy stand. So Junior took to asking me to watch his stand while he snuck away for ten or fifteen minutes for a smoke, bribing me with a soft drink or a praline. Junior was about fourteen or fifteen and good looking, but I was a cherubic eight year old with wispy platinum blonde hair and the innocence of a babe.

Cars started to stop just so old ladies could "oooh" and "aaah" over me, and they always bought something as an afterthought or an excuse. I started to sell the hell out of the stuff, and Junior thought that made him look good to Mrs. Kenny, so he started to let me come almost daily for a week or more. What neither of us knew was that Mrs. Kenny was no fool, and she began spying on the candy stand to see why the sales had gone up so much.

Ultimately, Mrs. Kenny came to my house and asked me to go to work for her selling pralines, telling me that Junior had left her. In my naivete, I accepted her offer, only to later learn, from an embittered but forgiving Junior Williams, that she had canned him.

Mr. Kenny was a roly poly Irishman and Mrs. Kenny was a roly poly Jewish lady. I don't know where Mr. Kenny had acquired his money, possibly from the real estate transactions he was involved in to some degree in the Bay, but the money came from Mr. Kenny and he adoringly spent it on Mrs. Kenny and whatever enterprise tickled her fancy, such as the antique store and praline business.

I was enthralled in being on 'the inside' of the business. As I picked up my stock in the kitchen each morning, I'd get to see the black ladies scooping the sugar from twenty gallon garbage cans into the large pots, dumping in the shelled pecans as the mixture caramelized, and then pouring the contents out on marble tables in approximate three inch circles to cool and harden. The thrill of mass production, the challenge of salesmanship, and the heavenly odor of it all.

Mrs. Kenny first employed me for the magnificent sum of eight dollars a week, which was seven eight hour days a week during my summer vacation. I took pride in seeing how much I could sell and started grossing $50 to $200 a day. It would have probably taken me much longer to reflect on the disparity between my salary and the dramatic increase in sales I had brought about, had Mrs. Kenny not been prone to pettiness in her bookkeeping, docking me for every missing or broken piece of candy returned, yelling shrilly at me for every error made, and giving me cause to believe that she was deliberately miscounting stock in her favor and at my expense. After two weeks I quit.

Mrs. Kenny came to my house and tried to intimidate me into coming back to work, yelling and screaming at me until Katherine interceded by asking Mrs. Kenny to leave. Katherine counseled me and, after hearing my frustration in dealing with such large sums of money and ending up with practically nothing after Mrs.

Kenny docked my pay, Katherine suggested that, if I enjoyed the work and the money, I might offer to work on commission. Mrs. Kenny dickered with me over the commission. I asked for 25%, she offered 3%. I asked for 20%, she offered 6%. Finally Mrs. Kenny figured out that I only understood fractions, but not percentages. To me, 25% was a fourth, 20% was a fifth, and so forth. Mrs. Kenny offered me 13.5%, knowing I could never compute it, and I returned to work for her making somewhat more than I had previously, but not what a fair count would have paid me. I knew damn dying well that 13.5% should be more than a tenth, but it rarely ever was when she counted it.

The 'praline stand' business was a tradition on Highway 90 along the entire Gulf Coast. In Bay St. Louis, Mrs. Kenny was not the only small businessman with praline stands, but she had the most strategically located ones. She owned the house on the beach corner at the foot of the bridge with a praline stand at that location, the first place westbound cars see after crossing the bridge, and she owned the one in front of the antique store a half block from the bridge, the next likely stop for a westbound car. Most tourists come from the East and all the other praline stands in the Bay were a half mile or more west of the bridge, so Mrs. Kenny was the Praline Queen of Bay St. Louis.

There was no little competition, though. There were a growing number of stands west of town, some even combining gift shops with candy sales and offering other inducements to customers. Halfway through the summer, Charley Benigno, a major contender for the market, heard of my salesmanship and frustration with Mrs. Kenny's bookkeeping, and offered me a job in his new stand with 20% commission and a roof over my head for rainy days. I took it, even though the extra inducement he offered customers was under the counter booze in a state that pretended to be dry. Even though I increased his candy sales, his location did not achieve the volume of sales Mrs. Kenny's did, but, with the added commission and added revenue from booze, even though it was a hard sell for an eight year old, I made more money and had far less grief than with Mrs. Kenny.

My first summer of employment was a huge success. I managed to take all the wrinkles out of my stomach almost all the time, even if it was accomplished with a high sugar diet of mostly candy and ice cream.

I even managed to save some money and become a banker to my sister and kids in the neighborhood who, inspired by my success, borrowed money to buy gumball punch cards. For a nickel, dime, or quarter a punch, the client would punch through the tissue paper covered circle to receive a gum ball and a folded piece of paper with a possible winning number on it. The lesser prizes were in larger punch out circles on the board such as pocket knives and fountain pens and Crackerjack type toys. The grand prizes were send away items like bicycles and such, though I never knew anyone to win a grand prize. The enterprising youngster, who bought the board for from one to five dollars from the local grocers and drugstores who sold them as a sideline, could double or triple their money by selling all the punches on the board.

My sister was a very aggressive salesman and did very well with them, although lending her the money was a losing proposition for me as she would use all her sales techniques, including an appeal to my sympathies and family loyalty, to get me to buy enough punches to negate her loan from me.

Though I continued to work part-time at the praline stand after school started in the fall, there came a time when seasonal rains and cold made it impractical. Then we had to scramble for other income. I would harvest the pecans from our four pecan trees in the back yard, but only one of them yielded 'paper shell' pecans with thin easy to remove shells and large fat meat inside. Those were easy to sell, but the harvest from one tree doesn't amount to much and the small hard shelled pecans from the other three trees brought even less.

At Christmas time, we would make our own tree decorations based on some of Katherine's original designs. One group of ornaments that always impressed people was a collection of five or six silhouettes of ballet dance figures cut out of cardboard, painted silver, and glittered on both sides. These would hang from a centered thread so they would spin or rotate with the slightest air convection, catching the light with their glitter and simulating pirouetting dancers. We also made angel dolls for the tree top starting with small inexpensive china dolls from the dime store and costuming them with silver and gold gilded and glittered wings and halos and crowns.

With the success of my praline sales career, we attempted a Christmas season door to door sales campaign of home made tree ornaments that met with enough limited success to warrant repeating the seasonal campaign for several years.

In turn, the limited success of the ornament sales led us to take a crack at street vending home made souvenirs on Highway 90. We took the hard shelled pecans no one would pay much for as an edible nut, painted faces on them, and put headgear and a miniature loop gold earring on them, the ear ring being the smallest size drapery ring. Half wore bandannas and had pretty faces to make them into black mammy heads. The other half had mustaches, eye patches, and pirates hats with hand painted skull and crossbones on them, the hats and eye patches made from remnants of black oilcloth. We hand lettered little cards that said, "I'm a lucky nut from Bay St. Louis" and they became our hottest selling souvenir items.

We also mimicked some of the other 'tourist

poison' in the highway gift shops such as glass ashtrays we'd paint scenes and legends on, figurines and night lights made of shells with legends spelled out in alphabet soup letters that were glued on and shellacked over, and costume jewelry made from tiny seashells and pearlized paint which we ordered the parts for from Florida wholesale houses, all of which we'd make by hand. Even Lo got into the act by hand sewing 'mammy dolls' which we sold in our souvenir lineup.

Katherine made me a box tray that hung from a strap around my neck and hooked onto my belt. I would sometimes be in competition against Mrs. Kenny's praline stands strolling the half block between the bridge and the antique store with my tray of souvenirs, and other times meeting the Greyhound Bus and the L&N (Louisville and Nashville) trains as they arrived at their respective stations. It was a hard sell and very discouraging in the cold and rainy winters, but it showed a minute profit that helped iron out the wrinkles in our stomachs.

The following summer I had a lot of offers to work for the praline stands, but a new challenge came my way that appealed to my sense of freedom and to my taste buds in a way that was to become a lifelong vice. A man named Patterson had just established a small ice cream manufacturing plant in nearby Waveland, and he offered me the position of, and I use his very words, "head of the sales division."

Of course, the 'sales division' consisted of me and one ice cream pushcart. He would deliver the goods to me and I would traverse most of the town by foot on hot and rainless days, pushing the cart on its three bicycle wheels and ringing the strand of sleigh bells strung between the push handle. I enjoyed the sense of being my own boss, and when I'd get tired I'd tell myself I was on a sightseeing tour. As with the pralines, I ate up a lot of my profits and developed a lifetime addiction to ice cream, but it proved as successful as previous enterprises and broadened my sense of accomplishment.

But selling ice cream outdoors is a very seasonal gig, and I was always searching for something I might sell that didn't involve all the hand work our tree ornaments and souvenirs required. Two factors led me into a brief career as an animal hunter, an enterprise which ultimately began to prey on my conscience.

The first factor was that Winter meant foraging for firewood in the surrounding swamps, and this meant learning how to avoid running afoul of snakes and alligators. My teacher in jungle lore might, in retrospect, have led to tragic consequences, because a hobo camping in the swamps is the nightmare of every parent concerned with child molestation. 'Bobo' was the name the town gave to a hobo who made Bay St. Louis his Winter home, and he traveled with a smaller quieter fellow who may or may not have been his significant other.

I had learned how to catch 'mud bugs' (crawfish) in the stream beds in the swamp. I was cooking some in a paint can I'd found over a campfire I'd made while foraging firewood. Bobo chanced upon me and, just before I was about to eat them, he cautioned me that I might be poisoning myself with lead from the paint can. He offered me some of the meal he and his companion had prepared. Hunger, curiosity, and the delicious aroma coming from a pot over his campfire led me to accept.

Tasting the bowl he proffered, I asked him what it was and how was it prepared. As he ladled out bowls for himself and his companion, he matter-of-factly said, "First you steal a chicken from a back yard, then you shoplift some dried lima beans and salt and cheesecloth. Dress the chicken, put it in the cheesecloth, put it in a pot with the beans and salt and water over a fire, and serve it two hours later." With that he opened the cheesecloth sack and spooned some of the chicken meat into my bowl.

Bobo was color blind, an advantage in spotting dangerous reptiles like snakes and alligators which camouflage renders invisible to us color sighted individuals. He taught me to look for the warm places these cold blooded animals picked to hide in wait for prey; a rock that retained the sun's warmth, or a log that blended with their camouflage pattern. He explained the movement and sounds that would reveal their presence, which snakes were poisonous and which were not, and the consequences of failing to distinguish between them.

To demonstrate the latter, he pulled up the pants leg of his companion to reveal a calf and lower thigh that had half the musculature surgically removed as the result of a snakebite from a cottonmouth moccasin. Holding the pants leg up, he said, "That's why he limps." Then he dropped the pants leg and closed his eyes, as if pained by the rumors he knew townspeople whispered about the two, "That's why he travels with me, so I can protect him." As Bobo opened his eyes and looked at me without malice, his companion turned his head and looked away.

The other factor that made me an animal hunter was being invited by a classmate to his family's farm for dinner. As his father showed me the barn, a big king snake slithered across the barn floor into the straw in the corner. I shouted, "Watch out, there's a snake."

The farmer smiled and said, "Don't fret, son, that's just George. He's a kingsnake and they ain't poisonous. He polices that barn for rats better than a rat terrier, and a damn sight better than those fat cats my wife overfeeds in the house."

I proudly responded, "Yes, Sir, I know. Someone told me they're not poisonous. They're kinda like a mini-boa constrictor." I was not sure about explaining Bobo as my source of information.

The farmer was impressed, "That's right, son. Hey, if you catch any of them fella's, me or one of my neighbors will pay you fifty cents apiece. But be careful, boy, and don't go picking up any rattlers or moccasins."

My snake hunting equipment consisted of a three-foot long stick with a fork at the end, a gunny sack to put them in, a machete to make my way through the swamp, and wrappings for my pants cuffs to keep insects and leeches from my legs and afford some protection from snakebite, because I couldn't afford boots.

The fork in the stick is placed behind the snake's head so he cannot strike while you pick him up with a firm, but not too firm, grip at that same point. You can use the stick to keep him more or less uncoiled while you maneuver him into the sack, otherwise he will coil around your arm and, if large enough and a constrictor like a kingsnake, can become a little uncomfortable and tricky to disengage.

Traipsing through those swamps I ran into a variety of misadventures from duplicating a scene from a Tarzan movie when I unwittingly stepped on the back of an alligator, thinking it was a log (he just gave me a dirty look and moved away slowly), to having the hell scared out of me by a snarling bobcat in a tree I got too close to. Amazingly, although I sidestepped numerous strikes by poisonous snakes, I never got a poisonous snake bite, although a kingsnake can deliver a nasty bite you'll remember.

I spent that entire season catching live kingsnakes for farmers. But, to my regret and shame, I elected to expand my profit margin by catching, killing, and skinning any colorful poisonous snake I found in my search for kingsnakes. The tourist shops on highway 90 would pay up to two dollars apiece for the fancy patterns of timber rattlers and water moccasins, depending upon their size, and the detached rattles themselves. They used the skins on belts and hatbands and sold the rattles as souvenirs in bins beside those with Indian arrowheads.

Despite my subliminal shame in snake hunting,

the neighborhood children were fascinated by my enterprise and I felt like a showman letting them see me transfer the kingsnakes from gunny sack to wood boxes for delivery.

Years later, working as a 'kidnapper' (baby photographer) in schools and churches up near Hamburg, I saw preachers in dirt floor churches doing their 'snake in the cane' bible routines with long iridescent black chicken snakes called blue runners, which I knew to be non-poisonous. Once one of them escaped the minister's hands and the line of children waiting to be photographed gasped as I calmly picked it up and returned it to him, and I was reminded of the kids who watched me handle the kingsnakes when I was but a child myself.

Katherine's disapproval of seeing the snake skins drying on boards hung from our garage rafters, Bobo's admonition that I shouldn't kill snakes unless I was going to eat them (didn't do that until decades later in the Orient), and my conscience pangs remembering the Rosicrucian literature I had read from Lo's archives, led me to abandon the enterprise before the next season rolled around.

By next winter I had to look around for indoor part time employment that was not dependent on tourists, good weather, or compromising my conscience.

There were two weekly newspapers in town, not that the town could support two papers. Only one, *The Sea Coast Echo*, actually had enough advertising in it to turn a profit or afford things like photo engravings. The other, *The Light,* was published by Mrs. Charmichael, a militant lady who delighted in giving the local politicians holy hell by detailing their peccadillos and questionable ethics in her small unglamourous paper printed in the dilapidated one story building she owned across the street from the court house.

Mrs. Charmichael was a touch eccentric, rather

short, stout, grey haired, and fortyish. She was not known as a fashion pate, and she was known to swear like a sailor on occasion. She had a large spider monkey for a pet and it could usually be seen chained to a small tree outside the front office of her newspaper building. On more than one occasion, the monkey would break its chain, particularly if frightened by dogs, and lead Mrs. Charmichael and her staff on a merry chase through a town filled with mature trees in which to swing back and forth.

I became one of Mrs. Charmichael's staff which consisted of Mr. Lederer, the printer who looked like the pedantic little old German man he was, and myself, the 'printer's devil.' A printer's devil is a janitor, a gofer, and an apprentice. When I was not sweeping the floors or fearfully feeding the monkey, I was cleaning the press and fonts, returning the hand set type and 'furniture' (type spacers) to their compartmented drawers, and hand feeding the gloppy ink on the rotating platen of the antique semi-motorized press as Mr. Lederer hand fed the very cheap and yellowish newsprint into it.

The Light had a very few brave and loyal advertisers, for Mrs. Charmichael was the avowed enemy of the local 'establishment.' The bulk of the paper, which was usually not bulkier than four to eight magazine sized pages, was primarily devoted to Mrs. Charmichael's voluminous editorials which would sometimes cap the description of a court scene with lines like, "And as I looked up at the Stars And Stripes hanging over the judge's head, I thought how much more appropriate it would be to fly the Jolly Roger."

My career as a printer's devil lasted until, not surprisingly, Mrs. Charmichael's print shop mysteriously caught fire one night. Although she rebuilt and resumed crusading against the inequities of small town politics, I had moved on to new summer employment.

Hearing of my work as a printer's devil, Uncle

Pete, Will Schmidt's brother who fell heir to Schmidt Brothers Engraving on Poydras Street in New Orleans, offered me a similar job in the engraving shop. Pete Schmidt, though not as talented nor as enterprising as his brother Will, was none-the-less a kind and competent man. White haired and round faced, he was always smiling and trying to please, whether it was his customers or his employees.

At this point in history, engraving was largely supplanted by the less expensive and more versatile printing technologies, but engraving was still the hallmark of the upper classes who judged others by whether their business cards, birth announcements, or wedding invitations were truly hand engraved or bourgeois enough to be printed. Engravers loathed hearing or using the term 'printing,' referring to their process as 'making an impression.' Anyone using the loathsome term, be they a new customer or a new employee, would be cooly reminded of the vast distinction between printing and 'making an impression.'

Printing in the 1940's was of the 'hot press' or 'raised type' variety, as opposed to today's 'offset' processes. With raised type, the positive metal image first comes in contact with the ink and then with the paper. This was made possible by the invention of the linotype machine and the photo-engraving processes. Text and images could be achieved quickly and accurately by these semi-automated processes. Prior to this, raised type had to be laboriously hand-set, as Mr. Lederer taught me at *The Light*, and images were mostly achieved through handcut wood blocks which endured only a limited run. Thus it had been since the Chinese invented printing in the 8th century and the Europeans advanced it in the 15th century.

But, concurrent throughout history and even pre-history, was the art of engraving, the act of carving an 'intaglio' or negative image in stone or metal. After the invention of paper, these 'engravings' were used to impress an image by first wiping ink into the recesses of the negative image, wiping off the excess ink from the flat plane of the stone or metal, and then impressing the paper with the plate which would leave its inky image on the paper. In ways a simpler and more direct transference of the image maker's creation to the finished product.

Some artists still use this process to make 'etchings' which can be hand reproduced in limited editions. It is also still used in the 'gravure' process which makes possible the color prints on cheap newsprint that you see in your Sunday magazine supplement. The plates from which they are produced are negative 'engravings' which, though semi-automatically produced as photo engravings, can transfer colored inks to cheap newsprint more accurately than raised type can.

I began in Uncle Pete's shop by making the business cards on the 'dumbbell screw press,' so called because of the two ball weights on its upper handle which, when spun, would drive the center screw down to press the paper against the engraving plate with a tremendous force. The plate would be inked and wiped by hand, the card hand placed in the frame, and the dumbbell spun the instant the other hand was clear. There was a fair percentage of paper waste in the process, certainly a lot of manpower waste, and an occasional mishap resulting in a lifelong deformity of a fingernail or missing finger. Fortunately, I progressed to more interesting things before experiencing such a mishap.

There were mechanized machines in the shop, but I was keenly interested in the actual creation of the plates, having seen my grandfather's elaborately hand engraved works in our home and marveling at the detail and precision that had gone into them. Uncle Pete put me on the pantograph, a device for transferring lettering from a large template onto the shellac coating of a copper plate. The scribe would scratch the letter through the shellac to the copper, after which an acid would more deeply etch the image into the copper. After the acid bath and an acid neutralizing bath, hand gravers would be used to 'clean up' the image under a magnifying glass. I considered this process cheating as compared to the work in my grandfather's time, but I learned there were few engravers left capable of keeping up with an apprentice's output on a pantograph, and there was no place for 'artistry' in a shop that was already losing ground rapidly to the print shops that surrounded us.

    I persevered through the summer in that overcrowded poorly ventilated shop, starting at 35 cents an hour and ending at 50 cents an hour, and tried to cling to the romantic image of artists creating beautiful multi-colored Mardi Gras engraved invitations and my ambidextrous grandfather churning out exquisite hand engravings with both hands simultaneously without the aid of a pantograph. But the only ones who shared my dreams were ghosts who shied away from the deafening clatter of the machines and the stench of the inkstained floor.

    Returning to the Bay, I again sought the environment of food, but, this time, the food was of a more balanced nutritional diet. Starting a couple blocks west of the bridge, Highway 90 was lined with a collection of 'tourist traps,' praline stands, gift shops, gas stations, and 'roadhouses,' eateries that were slightly less than a restaurant and slightly more than a hotdog stand.

    The closest thing to a restaurant in the collection was Mom's Café, owned and operated by Joe Church and his wife. Joe looked a lot like Gene Kelly and had the same kind of wholesome good Samaritan character about him. I guess Joe was French, not so much because his black hair was slicked back and he wore a little pencil line mustache, and not necessarily because he loved to cook and was great at it. I kind of got the impression he was French because of the way he responded to the whimsy of fate with a shrug of his shoulders and a wise 'wait and see' attitude.

Among the other fine foods he prepared, Joe's roast beef po' boy (poor boy) sandwiches were famous far and wide. With the affluence I had acquired in three years of more or less continuous employment, I had become an infrequent customer enjoying those delicious roast beef po'boys.

Joe offered me thirty-five cents an hour to be his dishwasher, which didn't actually compete with other options I had, but he threw in 'free meals,' and free meals prepared by Joe Church at Mom's Café was a considerable inducement. I happily washed dishes for Joe, hauled the beer cases out of the chilled storeroom where the steaks were hung up to age, and swept and mopped the linoleum tile floor with its black and white checkerboard pattern repeated in the checkered tablecloths. I learned the art of being a frycook on the grill I had to clean with a brick every night, how to prepare baked goods and salad dressings from scratch, and the secret ingredient of Joe's roast beef gravy that was the final touch to his famous po'boys. It was ground bone meal that came in glass jars from Carnation.

I also learned what a family was like when there was a loving caring father in the picture. Joe's beautiful French-Irish wife was taller than him even without the high heels she usually wore, a totally loving and supporting helpmate in his every endeavor, and the mother of his two beautiful little boys at that time. His sons received appropriate discipline generously balanced with approval and affection, and with them I experienced what it must be like to care for a younger sibling. For, if I could have chosen my own father, Joe Church would have been my idea of a perfect role model.

When business slacked off in the winter, I found another part-time job that paid very little, but fascinated me with a magical new area of technology. The local movie theater was called the A&G, established by the Ames and Gaspard families. Katherine told me that it originated around World War I as an open air theater on a wooden pier-like structure over the water on the Beach Road center of town. The white sheet screen would billow in the breezes off the bay and the silent hand cranked 16mm projector would make the same kind of jerky flickering images as the one Aunt Thelma sent us from Staten Island.

The 16mm hand-cranked Keystone projector Aunt Thelma sent with a dozen short reels of Disney animateds, Tom Mix westerns, and, my favorite, a green tinted underwater documentary of catching turtles in Florida, had been an extension of our fascination with 'magic lanterns.' We had two older magic lanterns, a kerosene burning one that had once belonged to great grandmother Mimi and used both circular and horizontal hand-painted glass slides from Germany, and an electrified 'dual' type that used horizontal glass slides in one direction and showed postcards as an opaque projector in the other direction. 'Magic Lantern Shows' were a regular part of our childhood entertainment, looking at the many postcards Will Schmidt had sent home from his European travels, and making up stories we would edit together from family photos put in the projector.

In one of my brief associations with the local Methodist Church, one Katherine had played the violin in on several occasions, I discovered there was a need for a slide projector to utilize educational film materials available to the church. I thought about applying the family magic lanterns to this need, but found the 35mm slide and filmstrip materials were not compatible with our old projectors.

I researched the appropriate equipment in New Orleans and bargained with an audiovisual dealer who, impressed with my youthful enterprise, provided me with an SVE (Society for Visual Education) Model AAA slide and filmstrip projector at an amazing discount. While I took little interest in the religious filmstrips I exhibited for the Methodist Sunday School, I discovered there was a great variety of other educational materials available in slides and filmstrips, and I began to collect a library of these materials.

When I was a child going to the A&G Movie Theater, it had moved across the street to the landward side of Beach Road and was a two-story high moderately ornate brick structure with the standard dual 35mm sound projection equipment of the day. I would pay my ten cents (a price which escalated a nickel at a time almost every year), sit in that darkened temple of imagination, and thrill to the sound of Charles Boyer's voice, tingle to the sexiness of Marlene Deitrich's moves, and root for the Indians when all my peers were cheering for Roy Rogers and Gene Autry.

I discovered that the fifty-gallon drum behind the theater was used to incinerate film scraps, and I took to going through the ashes to salvage bits of film which I would mount in hand made manilla slide mounts to use in my slide projector. I collected sets of ten or twenty related frames to tell the story of a movie or illustrate a particular category of subject, bathing beauties being one of my first and favorite categories.

The projectionist's name was Charles Zerr, a man who had once worked for Sam Goldwyn and who, after a life of drinking and working his way through the exhibitor's circuit, had married one of the Ames girls to settle down and help her spend her money, despite the interference of the elderly Mrs. Gaspard who tried to keep him from going through all of it. Mr. Zerr had mostly indulged himself by building and stocking an extensive bird aviary behind the beach house a block from the theater where he, his wife the former Miss

Ames, and Mrs. Gaspard resided.

Mr. Zerr had surreptitiously watched me salvage film from the incinerator before he accosted me one day to learn, to his surprise, what I was doing with it. Impressed by my interest in film, he offered me $15 a week to spend the hours between 7PM and midnight in the projection booth with him where I would clean up, go fetch him coffee from The Hamburger Heaven across the street in quart glass milk bottles with lots of cream and sugar, rewind the big 2000 foot 35mm reels and splice in the commercials to the 'Extra Added Attractions' reel, and learn how to adjust the 'carbon-arc' lamp house of the two projectors before the changeover from one reel to the next. The clincher was that I would be allowed to sit in the balcony, the unused half opposite the black patron's segregated balcony, and watch the movies when he didn't need me.

This is how I first became a film devotee, studying the technology and dynamics of film making by viewing five or more films a week, hundreds and hundreds of films throughout the decade of the forties. Even after I no longer worked for Mr. Zerr, he and his wife would give me rolls of tickets as a birthday or Christmas present because they knew they were responsible for making me a film addict.

By the time I entered highschool, my interest in film and photography had expanded to the point that I wanted to learn more of the technology. I asked Lo if I could stay with her in the summers so I could seek work in the film processing plants there to learn more about photography. I found work at Bennett's Photofinishing Plant, the largest such plant in the South and owned by the same family that owned Bennett's Photo Store, the largest photo store in the South.

The plant was on the third floor of a building a block from the store. When materials were needed, I would fetch them from the store, which gave me an opportunity to familiarize myself with the equipment and operation of the photo retail business. The plant itself was an excellent and thorough indoctrination into the technology of photography, far far exceeding my brief experience with Mr. Cape on Staten Island.

The plant was mostly staffed with women, the only other two males being Mr. Ventola, the manager, and a young hunchback man who obviously was the brains of the operation and was constantly pulling Mr. Ventola's fat out of the fire. Mr. Ventola, though handsome, was married, so I, although I was years younger and much more naive than I appeared, got a lot of assistance and attention from the two dozen women who worked there.

I worked in every facet of the operation from the film processing room (entirely manual in those days), to the film finishing room, the enlarging room, the washers, the sorting and bagging department, and, the most thrilling, the printing room. There's something very stimulating to the male ego to be the only man in a darkened red-lighted room with eight or ten women who spend eight hours a day talking about their lives, their loves, and their libidos.

Most of the printing machines were automated to the extent of having automatic exposure, and the women mastered these easily and operated them repetitiously without boredom or frustration. The contact printers and one or two specialty printers, such as 35mm half frames, required a human's arbitrary exposure calculation and few of the women could or would bother to operate them. When I worked in the printing room, I would operate these arbitrary exposure devices, manually placing each exposed print on one of the two conveyor belts which the other machines automatically fed to until the prints dropped in one of the two huge trays at the end of the conveyor where two girls in rubber gloves would process and pass the prints onto the automatic rocker washers. If a print stained or was too far off acceptable exposure, the girl at the tray would inform that respective operator to do a makeover based on the code number on the back of each print.

During lunchtime, the girls would gratefully leave the printing room for a breath of fresh air and camaraderie in the light of day. I would sometimes take advantage of this time to catch a nap by lying on the conveyor belt in the relaxing darkness and quiet of the red lighted room.

There was one very attractive lady who bitterly complained about her boyfriend going to prison and leaving her six months pregnant. She still looked very sexy despite her protruding belly the day she declined to leave the printing room at lunch time and, instead, came over to where I lay on the conveyor belt and leaned over me provocatively.

If I had not been so very young, naive, and a little frightened, that moment would surely have been my initiation into manhood. Even the lady's brushing her breasts across my face and fondling me through my clothing did not overcome my mounting fear. Not only was I not initiated into manhood that day, but it served to make me the focus of many jokes thereafter about my virginity.

I learned more and more with each new job I acquired. I learned not only about the technology and dynamics of the job itself, but also about interpersonal relationships, economics, and, most of all, my own personal capacity to attempt anything I set my mind to and to obtain whatever means were necessary to advance to a new level of learning.

Hunger gave me the courage to go to work when I was eight years old. Job success gave me the means to buy a drum when I was ten, a piano when I was eleven, and a press camera when I was thirteen. In the years since, I have fulfilled far more goals than I have faced insurmountable ones, but never did I assume any goal was insurmountable until I had given it a damn good try.

My advice to one and all, no matter how young or how old you are, never let them tell you it can't be done. Nobody knows that until they themselves have tried.

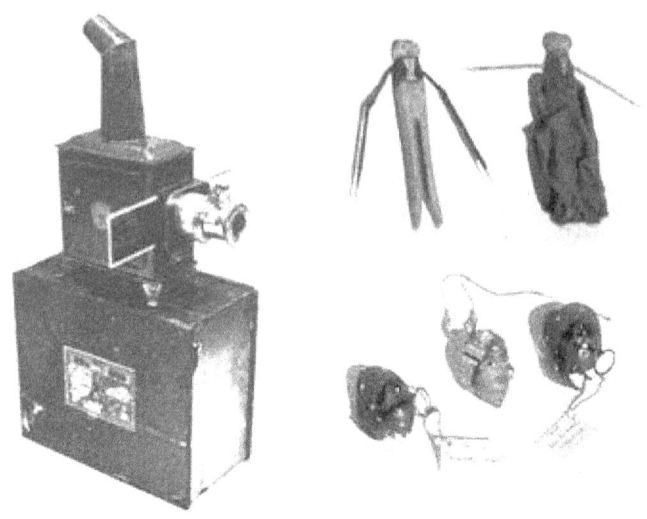

Mimi Stanselle's oil burning magic lantern, seen at left with its hand painted German glass slides, began the author's interest in graphic arts. Later the family's electric magic lantern projected his Grandfather's postcards from his travels in Europe with an emphasis on art and architecture. With his earnings, at ten he purchased a slide/filmstrip projector which led to working in the projection booth of the local theater, which led to a career in photography and cinematography. The author's first job, merchandising praline candy on the highway, led to selling ice cream from a push cart, and, in the off seasons, selling home made tourist items and Christmas decorations. These evolved from Katherine's WPA crafts, such as the clothespin dolls and annealed metal and bottle glass mosaics in photos. The pecan heads, glittered pirouetting ballet dancers, angels, cherubs, butterflies, and shadow portraits sold sufficiently to augment their $25 a month rental and WPA income.

Chapter Eight
THE WAR YEARS

About a year after our return to the Bay, early in 1941, the tenants moved out of the corner house and we reclaimed our former residence which now had electricity. Even so, our phonograph was still an old totally acoustic machine which required frequently changing the steel needles, winding the spring wound motor with a large crank on the side, and adjusting the wooden louvers that acted as a volume control for the internal folded acoustic horn that emanated through the louvers. The records were all heavy old 78 rpm's, some of them impressed only on one side, and consisted mostly of Caruso singing opera, Souza playing marches, and pop artists of the 1920's and 30's such as Al Jolson, Eddie Cantor, and Nick Lucas.

The Rochain's house, on the other corner of 2nd and St. George Streets, was sold and essentially rebuilt into a modern white cottage by the new family, the Burrows. Joe Burrow was working his way up in the administration of the Merchant's Bank, the newer of the two banks in town, and his wife, Lisa, became a close friend of Katherine. Their daughter was my age and their son a year or two younger. Joe was affluent, compared to most of the neighborhood, and they enjoyed such luxuries as a new powerful radio he played too loud for the neighbor's comfort on the open air side porch, and newer records which, when they were tired of them, we fell heir to. So Benny Goodman, Stan Kenton, and Billie Holiday joined our record collection.

The more established families on the block consisted of the Kergosin's on the corner of Carrol and 2nd who owned the drugstore on the beach at the head of Main Street, and the Cajun family across the street led by the matriarch, Mrs. Tokay. Mrs. Tokay had three daughters; Livinia who taught the 2nd grade at our school and who remained unmarried, Vanderlie who was a clerical worker in civic administration and later married, and Elsie who married Mr. Sellier and had five or six children through the years, the oldest a girl my age. Other families came and went in the half dozen other houses on those two blocks of 2nd Street.

In addition to the phonograph, we had Lo's old table radio with its' gothic shaped wooden cabinet and little orange lighted dial, a gift from Lo now that we had electricity. It was a sunny December morning that was so nice I thought about attempting some highway souvenir sales, when I heard someone at the Sellier's yelling out into the street that the President was about to make a radio speech.

We all clustered around the Gothic table radio to hear F.D.R. (President Franklin Deleno Roosevelt) make the historic speech that began, "Yesterday, December 7th, 1941, a day which will live in infamy, the United States of America was suddenly and deliberately attacked by naval and air forces of the Empire of Japan."

Everyone in the neighborhood had their radios turned up full volume so those without radios could hear the broadcast. It was like the whole neighborhood was in one big living room sharing the momentous broadcast. The broadcast prompted various reactions ranging from children failing to grasp its' significance to some of the adults indulging in mild hysteria and contemplating immediate air attacks and beach invasions by both German and Japanese forces.

The next few days everyone was in mild shock, slowly adjusting to the idea that air attacks and invasion landing parties were not imminent. Radio commentators concentrated on rehashing the recent history of American-Japanese peace negotiations intended to avert war, and the stone-walling of Japanese emissaries who successfully deceived American negotiators to veil the intended attack on Pearl Harbor. The commentators also reviewed the history of the war in Europe which most Americans favored staying out of before Pearl Harbor was attacked. The naivete of such head in the sand neutrality was blown away with the ships in Pearl Harbor.

Within the first few weeks, however, the movie newsreels brought the reality of a modern shooting war within sight and sound of every citizen, and the reaction was polarized between those who reacted with a blind patriotic zeal and those who sank into a fatalistic doomsday attitude.

The patriots themselves were polarized between negative and positive reactions. The negative reactionaries in cities like New Orleans painted swastika graffiti on the windows of German businesses and stoned Mr. Hanada's shop on Royal Street, jeering as he and his family were removed by the authorities to be relocated in a detention camp for the duration of the war. In Bay St. Louis they simply began rather absurd rumors about families of recent German descent and one utterly ridiculous story about an elderly couple from France being spies simply because they spoke with a heavy accent.

The positive patriots organized parades soliciting young men to enlist in the armed forces and, after the government got organized with its' war programs, promoting War Bond sales and the collection of salvage materials.

First there were the scrap metal drives, starting with the World War I cannon on the Court House lawn. Weekly trucks scoured the town collecting every metal scrap citizens would freely donate from flattened tin cans to broken pots and pans and toys and whatever, all of which was dumped in a huge bin built around the Court House cannon. In those days, tin foil had more lead in it than today and was used in the wrappers of all candy bars, cigarettes, and as the liner in all boxed foodstuffs. Saving tin foil was particular fun for candy eating kids who would roll the tin sheets into balls, competing to see who could create the biggest ball of tin foil before donating it.

Explosives of that day used glycerin as a prime ingredient, and another national salvage drive was initiated to get housewives to save and donate their used cooking oils, the newsreels giving instructions on how to pour exhausted cooking fats into large tin cans and cap them with waxed paper or tin foil lids secured with string or rubber bands. In all these endeavors, our little household felt rather guilty because we had very little in the way of excess oil or tin cans or tin foil.

On War Bond Drives we broke even, however, as we compensated for our inability to buy bonds with our artistic ability to make posters and provide music. Many a night we all labored over 22 inch by 28 inch manilla poster boards with our red, white, and blue poster paints making War Bond posters, and many a time we'd proudly listen as Katherine's violin sang out at War Bond rallies, "Any bonds today, bonds of freedom, that's what I'm selling for the U.S.A.."

But there were times when we were the depressed ones, if not exactly doomsday fatalists like some of the older folks. We felt somewhat guilty that we had so little to give to the war effort. The government inaugurated a War Bond Stamp system so school children could buy the stamps to put in a book which they could trade in for a $25 war bond when filled. I started such a book with my intermittent earnings, but I could never compete with my school peers whose parents bought them $25 bonds as frequently as I could buy a handful of stamps. We were painfully aware that my stamp gesture was pathetic, our salvage materials were pitifully few, and we had no adult male family member in the Armed Forces.

Movie newsreels were at least half government propaganda, apart from the special propaganda films that replaced the *Selected Short Subjects* that used to accompany the cartoon before the feature. And much of this propaganda imparted a sense of guilt if you did not contribute adequately and regularly to the war effort. Almost every house in our neighborhood had silver stars hanging in their windows to indicate they had a man in service, and some of these were replaced by gold stars to symbolize that man had died in service.

Our uncomfortable feeling was compounded with the initiation of rationing. Gas, food, shoes, and a great variety of what was considered 'essentials' were only available if you had the appropriate 'coupons' in your 'ration book.' Most of these were items we could not afford anyhow, so the fact that we always had excess ration coupons and our friends and neighbors were always in need of them brought home the disparity between our lifestyle and what was considered 'normal.'

Our '39 Plymouth, that had taken us to and from Staten Island, had been resigned to the tin garage behind the house because we couldn't afford gas for it even at ten and fifteen cents a gallon. With the advent of the war, production of civilian cars and tires for same ceased, and without needed tires we were not likely to use it for the duration of the war. Still, in a sense of pride or family loyalty I did not understand then nor since, Katherine declined many profitable offers to sell the car simply because Aunt Thelma had paid for it and one does not sell a gift. Given our circumstances, I also could not agree with her ethics which kept her from getting a gas ration book for the car which could have been bartered profitably. It would have been much the same as the many meat and sugar ration stamps we gave freely to our neighbors because, usually, we could not afford such commodities, at least not in the quantities the government deemed essential.

All three of we children appeared older than our years, partly the precocity of our genes and partly the maturity imposed by the lessons of being 'genteel poor.' The war years fell the hardest on A.J. who was only sixteen when the war began, but appeared to be old enough to join the service. Many assumed he was a 'draft dodger' or '4F,' meaning unfit for military service, which became a reality as soon as he was of age and rated 4F when he attempted to enlist.

A.J. not only appeared older, he sounded older by virtue of the early and extensive home schooling he had received from a private tutor in Canada who taught him to read years before his chronological peers. As a very young child he was educated in English history and acquired a lifelong interest in the knights of old and their Viking and Norman origins. By the age of seven he had read all the works of Shakespeare in the family library. Also at the age of seven he had surgery on both elbows to free fused joints, acquired a fascination with medicine, and by the age of ten had read all of his grandfather's medical books.

Like his grandfather, who's artistic talents had led him to illustrate some of the medical texts of his day, A.J. began to trace the medical drawings in the books in order to teach himself the principals of anatomy and biology. He dissected frogs and lizards, pickling them in bottles of formaldehyde, and when one of our pet dogs died, he got Katherine's permission and removed the animal's heart so skillfully that the glass bottled specimen brought impressive and sincere accolades from every doctor who viewed it.

A.J. read and in ways mimicked the intellectual wits of that time, mostly members of the Algonquin Roundtable such as Alexander Wolcott, Robert Benchley, and Dorothy Parker. He acquired a sardonic wit, the English art of understatement, and a rueful fondness for double entendre. With an almost photographic memory, he memorized the quips from the humorous novels of Thornton Wilder and he would append lines like "As the Bishop said to the Countess" or "As the Countess said to the Bishop" wherever it would change the context of your innocent remark into risque humor.

At the age of sixteen, A.J. had been drinking for three years. In his black felt jacket, brown Fedora, and sporting a briar pipe, he was not questioned in bars which pre-dated the legal drinking age laws and operated in open violation of state laws claiming Mississippi to be a dry state. In retrospect, I often wonder where he got the money to drink when we were literally destitute, but, I suspect, Katherine indulged what she suspected was one of the few affectations of manliness available to him, but which I suspect he viewed as sophistication.

As you travel East of New Orleans on Highway 90, you pass through sixty miles of small islands divided by rivers and swamps which separate Lake Ponchatrain from the Gulf of Mexico. This network of waterways is what makes Lake Ponchatrain the worlds largest salt water lake, constantly exchanging the salt water of the Gulf with the fluctuation of the tides. Bay St. Louis is the first town where Highway 90 meets he coastline and, for 18 miles East of the Bay, it hugs the beautiful white sand beaches which were created around the turn of the century by dredging up offshore sand to create a shipping channel known as 'the intercoastal waterway.' A stepped seawall helps retain the beach, which insures the tourist industry that flourishes along that particular section of coast.

Traveling East from the Bay, you pass through Henderson Point, Pass Christian, Gulfport, Mississippi City, and enter Biloxi before the Highway 90 veers inland and you lose the scenic beach drive. Two military bases sprang up, or rather expanded, along this coast.

Keesler Field in Biloxi became an Army Air

Force Base specializing in electronics training for Air Force personnel. They wore the usual army khaki uniforms, but were distinguished by brass insignia on their lapels of wings with an airplane prop in the center. They came from everywhere, including people like Neil Simon who immortalized his misadventures there in his production, *Biloxi Blues*.

The other base grew from the Merchant Marine Academy located in Henderson Point directly across the bay from Bay St. Louis. Here the Navy created a training and deployment center for its' 'Seabees,' the Navy's equivalent of the Army Corps of Engineers, responsible for all Navy land based construction and engineering projects. The Seabees wore regular navy blues, but were distinguished by an embroidered emblem of a smiling honeybee wearing a sailor cap and mischievously winking one eye. The Seabees were also distinguished by a reputation for being more outrageous than the milder mannered young men from Keesler.

The influx of Seabees in the Bay St. Louis bars was understandable, given the proximity of the base. But it's a safe guess that most of the Keesler boys who showed up in the Bay did so because of the desperately poor ratio of women to men in the areas surrounding Keesler Field.

This was an area poor by national standards to begin with, and further economically stressed by the national depression. Even with the relatively small pay for servicemen at that time, they were economically competitive with the local males for the attention of the ladies. Added to this was the material advantages of Military Post Exchanges supplying luxuries unavailable on the civilian market, the glamour of the uniform, and the romantic image of men who would very possibly face death in defense of their country.

A.J. had a penchant for bringing home stray dogs. He was the one who brought home Mooch, the double jointed ice eating mongrel who sprawled in our New Orleans living room with his limbs askew and his head on A.J.'s thigh. He brought home a part dalmatian mongrel we named Napoleon after a large spotted dog in the comic strips who looked just like him. All of his life, A.J. had a weakness for bringing home stray dogs and cats.

Perhaps this tendency was partly at work when A.J. frequented the bars in Bay St. Louis and found himself the first in our family to rub elbows with that varied assortment of servicemen who I'm sure appreciated his congenial company, his lack of resentment for their competitive presence, and the welcome news that he had a single mother and teen aged sister at home.

The first of them he brought home was a trio of Seabees, the oldest of whom was a married man around Katherine's age who A.J. nicknamed 'Chaos' because he was the rowdiest and most adventurous of the three. We good naturedly shared what little we had with them, and they were gratefully appreciative of our efforts, despite their surprise at finding a dirt poor family in the home of the cultured and educated young man who befriended them.

Chaos set his sights for Katherine who, knowing he was married, was constantly interjecting me bodily between the two of them, when even my innocence could sense the thinly veiled lust in his eyes. The youngest of the trio set his sights for my sister, Thelma, whose appearance and behavior belied her tender age of thirteen.

Katherine's WPA salary was increased to $40 a month and her talents now applied to decorating the USO (United Service Organizations) Clubs along the coast where servicemen went to socialize, hopefully with the local ladies. In time we got to see most of her work in the many clubs along the coast; huge service emblems many feet in diameter adorning the walls, festooned decorations in papers and fabrics of all kinds, and entertainment programs that often included her violin performance in solo or in ensembles. The USO club in the Bay was housed in the Knights of Columbus Hall and was where we met most of the servicemen we came to know.

One fellow was nicknamed Slovak because he was Czechoslovakian, and he taught us how to make goulash. Another asked us to house his thoroughbred English Bulldog for the duration of his stay at Keesler as he was not allowed to keep him on base. We most remember this ferocious looking but sweet and gentle dog named Turk for his habit of chasing after butterflies. One day he mistakenly chased a bee who stung him on his nose and poor Turk had to lay on his back in an effort to rub his deeply receding nose in the dirt for relief.

Forty-one at the beginning of the war, Katherine was still a very attractive woman and got more than her share of attention. One of her most persistent suitors was actually named Captain Corn. He was shorter than she, allegedly unmarried, and seemed to have more money to flash than a Captain's salary would provide, and flash it he did. He was very dictatorial in behavior, critical of all around him, and had the annoying habit of trying to bribe us children to obtain privacy with Katherine. As much as Katherine was turned off to sex and, all the moreso by Captain Corn's manners, she felt it was unpatriotic to totally reject a serviceman's entreaties. We children ran interference for her when Captain Corn's advances got too hot and heavy in the living room. It wasn't until fellow servicemen dredged up enough research on him, revealing he had an oil-rich Indian wife in Oklahoma, that Katherine felt justified in dropping him altogether.

There were others who woo'd her, some quite impressive, and more than one proved to be married despite their initial claims to be single. In those days, most men Katherine's age were married, and stayed married. And then there was Francis.

Francis Wilson was a short Italian man with a sturdy body, unimpressive features, and a quiet unassuming nature. He had curly dark brown hair, a large nose, and cocker spaniel eyes with long lashes. He had been raised in a Catholic orphanage, had a partner in a Detroit auto repair shop before entering the service, and worked as a mechanic in the motor pool at Keesler Field. He courted Katherine with patience, gentleness, and a degree of sensitivity and consideration that is rare among men. If not the man of most women's dreams, he nonetheless had the essential qualifications to scale her wall of inhibitions.

My sister Thelma, however, did not have to overcome such inhibitors as Lola's cloistered upbringing and Erle's ineptitude as a husband. Here was adolescence in full bloom amidst a sea of hungry men against the dramatic backdrop of America at war. She started with the young Seabee who was so good looking even I thought he was cute, and progressed through a succession of very attractive young men that she was too immature to appreciate and too inexperienced to know what to do with.

Thelma was born with an ectomorphic frame, a thin wiry body which most resembled Uncle Ezra, her father's father, and which she maintained into mid-adolescence. In her adult life she resembled Katherine's side of the family in face and figure, but her personality remained faithful to her father's family from early childhood through adolescence. This included a drive which Katherine rationalized as an 'overactive thyroid,' but which was so compulsive as to sometimes blind her to logic and sensitivity to others.

She learned from early exposure to her father the powers of manipulation and intimidation, and she exercised them beyond any rational need to assert her position in the pecking order of siblings. She learned very early that, as a child, I had a very low threshold of uncontrollable hysterical anger, and she delighted in almost daily driving me over that threshold until I would perform what the family called my 'Donald Duck act;' turning red in the face, becoming incoherent, and attacking my sister with homicidal intent. Of course, Thelma could run faster than I and was always safe, until one day when I picked up a nearby machete in my rage and gave chase. Thelma tripped and I would have caught and probably killed her had Katherine not, by great good fortune, been near enough to grab my clothing and restrain me until Thelma could escape.

Her techniques included conning me out of any money or material I possessed, alienating my peers and play friends usually by precipitating my uncontrollable rage for them to witness, and setting up A.J., myself, or anyone handy as a fall guy in her nefarious schemes. If anyone possessed more than she, she would not rest until she had acquired it from them. If anyone drew more attention than she, she would affect every guile she knew until she upstaged them. If anyone appeared more worthy than she, she would find their Achilles heel and defame them. She was invincible, and intolerable.

She had short thin 'dishwater blonde' hair, round questioning eyes, a cute button turned up nose, and classic dimples and cleft chin. As a child it all appeared as waif-like innocence. As an adolescent changing into an adult, her face passed for 'cuteness' and her figure slowly blossomed into an outrageous provocativeness.

While Katherine viewed Thelma's dating servicemen with fear for her chastity, A.J. and I recalled her manipulation of us as her early exercises in power, and we now viewed her toying with the affections of these boys as a game of cat and mouse. Not unlike many women, Thelma was only interested in them until they were hooked, after which she abused them, held them in disdain, and made herself attractive for the next victim.

The first two years of the war were not filled with the fun and games or heroic successes most theatrical films usually paint. The allies lost ground steadily in both the European and Pacific 'theaters of war,' and the grisly reality of death and destruction was viewed weekly in the movie newsreels.

There was an elderly man in the Bay who had been a Confederate soldier and was considered eccentric because he would never enter a building with an American flag on it, even hobbling to the other side of the street with his cane rather than walk in front of the Court House or any building that represented Federal authority. The explanation was that, during the Civil War, his pregnant wife had been disemboweled by a Union soldier wielding a bayonet while looting his unprotected home.

Some people were skeptical of the story, but they and I thought of it when we saw newsreels of captured Japanese footage showing Chinese babies ripped from their mother's arms and thrown in the air to be impaled on the bayonets of grinning Japanese soldiers. In the desperate years of the war, the government found it expedient to reveal the unbelievable atrocities of Japanese and German forces, but, after the war, they went to great lengths for several decades to suppress all record of them in order to economically rebuild their former enemies.

Not surprisingly, the bitter stories of male, female, and child prisoners of war did not find free expression until enough decades had passed for those former enemies to become formidable and sometimes ruthless competitors in the economic and political battlefields of the latter part of the century.

More and more servicemen from the Bay died in combat and the silver stars in the windows of their families turned to gold. *Colliers Magazine* began to run covers illustrated by an outstanding artist who had survived a German concentration camp and, in bitter response to his horrifying experiences, rendered elaborately illuminated drawings of the Axis leaders as the vilest and most evil of humans, their apparel and props and settings decorated with or related to skulls and bones and the morbid deathly images of the concentration camps. The image of and a preoccupation with death became the theme of nightmares and a reality even in the lives of children.

A young couple rented the next door cottage. The nice young man had brought his wife to the sunny seaside resort to try to overcome her condition of 'melancholia.' They had waited several years before succeeding in having the baby they so desired. The young wife had been bathing their beautiful healthy infant when the doorbell rang and she answered it briefly and immediately returned to her child, only to discover the baby had drowned in the bathtub. The sunny seaside resort did not noticeably improve the young woman's massive depression and, while the husband left her briefly to go to the grocery, she found a small caliber rifle in the house and blew her brains out.

Katherine was as concerned about me helping clean up the mess as I was about her being there, but, together, Katherine, Francis Wilson, and I cleaned it up without undue trauma. Francis explained matter-of-factly to me how the brain is contained in the skull cavity in a liquid under pressure, which explained why its' remains could cover such a large area when the pressure is suddenly released.

Katherine had befriended a country woman who had moved into a little house on State Street about three blocks away. Pansy Benoit was a good woman who resembled Lo in her younger years when her hair was black and her figure not quite so stout. Pansy used to entertain us with her homespun poetry which her limited education did not keep from being witty and wise.

One night she was walking home past the front of our house in the darkness of a 'blackout' (mock air raid drill). She hailed us while we sat on our front porch, and she continued on her way. Suddenly we heard her pained voice call out Katherine's name, and we ran to find her collapsed on the sidewalk. We carried her to the front porch and put her on the wicker chaise lounge, Francis and I holding her up on either side. Francis felt her left side contract and grow cold, and he said, "I think she's having a stroke." Afraid to move her, Katherine made us carry her on the chaise lounge the block and a half to the 'hospital,' a makeshift clinic operated in a small house around the corner on Carrol Avenue, where she was pronounced dead on arrival.

We did not become hardened to death. We still knew how to cry for the very real loss it represented. We cried for Pansy Benoit, and the little mother with melancholia, and for the young servicemen, both from the Bay and from the neighboring bases, who we had known personally, some of whom we learned were never coming back from war.

A.J. graduated from high school, was rejected for military service when he tried to enlist, and finally a last appeal was made to his father to assist him in entering Louisiana State University in Baton Rogue where he wanted to study medicine. Erle had made such promises off and on for years during his irregular annual brief visits while he was gathering tropical plant stock for his floral business in Canada. He would try to woo and bed Katherine with promises of financial support, medical support, educational support, and little would come of it.

I remember one time when we were house sitting for the Goldman's. A.J. and I stayed in one room and Katherine and Thelma in another. Then Erle arrived in town and paid a visit. Thelma was sent to stay in the room with A.J. and I that night. Years later when I was an adult, Katherine confessed she had succumbed to Erle's entreaties that night. There had been talk of reconciliation, even though Erle had been living with Norah, his common-law wife, for years. Erle promised Katherine the moon before bed-time. After bed-time, however, his tactic was to inform Katherine that all she had to do was to come to Canada and throw Norah out herself. I remember waking up that night as an angry Katherine got into bed with me and Erle was nowhere to be found in the morning.

But when the appeal was made for Erle to fulfill his promises of paying A.J.'s way into college, his response was for Katherine to send A.J. there and Erle would pay the tuition directly to the school. A.J. arrived in Baton Rogue, tentatively registered, settled into a dorm, and even signed up for ROTC (Reserve Officers Training Corps). Schools were much more trusting then and they allowed A.J. to remain for a month or two before it became obvious that Erle had no intention of paying the school's tuition. A.J. left in a sea of embarrassment.

Next A.J. took a job at the shipyards in nearby Pascagoula. He made good money for the first time in his life and seemed to like the freedom and the pride of being able to help Katherine financially. However, one little aspect of his education and sophistication proved disastrous. He had acquired the habit of swearing in Nordic terminology borrowed from his familiarity with the Vikings. Whenever he hit his thumb with the hammer it was Thor this and Oden that, and it all sounded like German to his redneck co-workers at the shipyard. A few of the bully-cum-vigilante types decided he was a German spy and took it upon themselves to beat the truth out of him. After A.J. got out of the hospital, he recuperated at home in the Bay for a while before deciding to look for work in New Orleans.

Erle's involvement in A.J.'s abortive attempt to

enter L.S.U. was the most our family had to do with him for some years, but it touched off a growing correspondence between Thelma and him. It began with the tack that, if he were to be supportive of any of his children, his first and principal interest was in Thelma, his favorite. It widened to become inquisitive about Katherine's growing relationship with Francis Wilson, the quiet mechanic in the Army Air Force at Keesler. And it grew to a climax when Erle was forced by his common-law wife, Norah, to bring her teenage daughter by a previous marriage into their home. Erle decided he wanted Thelma to come live with him in Canada. What no one in our family knew was that Erle and Norah were entering a period of severe alcoholism at that time.

Francis proposed marriage to Katherine, and she was undecided. She asked Lola, and Lo had become too democratized to find fault with Francis' social or economic status, and she could find no fault in him as a man. Katherine asked Dr. Horton, and Dr. Horton told her that a good man was healthy biological medicine as well as an asset to a family. She asked Euall Samples, the local Methodist Minister who our family liked because, despite the fact that none of us were committed to any particular religion, Euall did not proselytize and treated all with a non-sectarian approach that was rare among clergy, and all the rarer from the 'country boy' that he was. She told Euall, as she had the others, that her most important concern was the welfare of her children, and Euall told her that her happiness was as deserving and important as the happiness of any other member of her family.

She asked each of us children, and A.J. and I found no fault with Francis and urged her to follow her heart. Thelma, influenced by Erle's jealousy of Francis, was less supportive and, when Katherine agreed to marry Francis, Thelma elected to go live with her father, and Katherine did not stop her.

Katherine and Francis were married at the home of the Goldmans in the Spring of 1945 when the yellow roses covered the fence along Second Street where it curved toward the oyster factory on the beach. Katherine's hair was naturally brown by then and she wore a rose colored lace dress and heels that made her appear a half foot taller than Francis. Her many friends and family were truly happy for her.

Within days and in the first few weeks following their marriage, it became obvious that Katherine had consummated their union only after the marriage, because she became a changed woman literally overnight. She smiled for no obvious reason, she adopted a positive outlook on everything, and she accepted her own worthiness as a woman as well as a human.

Later she confessed to us that she had never experienced orgasm before or during her life with Erle, had been resigned to sex as an unwelcome obligation when she anticipated marrying Francis, and was dramatically surprised when the biological magic she never knew existed occurred on her wedding night with Francis.

The war had turned in favor of the Allies. Though we still sang *Once In A While* ("Once in a while, will you try to give one little thought to me ... ") and wistfully thought of the boys we had known who weren't coming back, the choking fulfillment of the song *White Cliffs of Dover* ("There'll be blue birds over, the white cliffs of Dover, tomorrow, when the world is free") finally came to pass, and, by the end of the year, the war was over.

Top: *(left to right)* Francis, Alfred, Chaos, Cutie Pie, Thelma, and Swede.

Center: author on WWII P40 fighter plane used as 'jungle gym' on schoolyard circa 1943.

Bottom: *(left to right)* Jeanie, Thelma, Johnny, author, and Tex. Jeanie and Thelma dated these two soldiers from Keesler Field. Jeanie married Tex. Thelma dumped Johnny, much to Katherine's regret.

Top: Chase cartoon from New Orleans Item dated 2/2/39 and autographed to Lola Schmidt, depicts Hitler and Mussolini keeping all of Europe dancing a nervous jig because Nazi Germany had just annexed Austria and Czechoslovakia and would 6 months later invade Poland, precipitating World War II.

Bottom: *(left to right)* AJ, Lo, Francis, Katherine, and author. The outdoor wedding took place at the home of Commodore and Mrs. Goldman.

Chapter Nine
MY EARLY ARTISTIC CAREER

Art and music had always been a part of our home, and a part of our family. Will Schmidt, in addition to being an engraver who carved beautiful illuminated designs freehand in copperplates with steel hand engravers, had a hobby of creating beautifully detailed renderings in pencil, charcoal, and pen and ink of scenes from his travels in Europe and whatever caught his eye. His letters to his daughters in boarding school often included "The Patton Street Gazette," a pen and ink hand rendered publication with profusely illustrated humorous stories of the goings on at home and in the neighborhood.

When the Tulane Medical School opened a training section on one of the upper floors of the building Will's shop was in, one of the medical students took him up to show him what it was all about, expecting him to faint at the sight of cadavers. To his surprise, Will took out pencil and paper and started to make illustrations of the revealed anatomy that fascinated him. Ultimately, he illustrated medical books and applied the art in his own medical practice years later.

Katherine had inherited his artisan's love of design and metal. She studied art academically, but remembered most fondly the days she apprenticed in the artisan shops around her father's engraving firm on Poydras Street in downtown New Orleans. The china painting was more of a hobby craft taught women of good breeding to keep themselves occupied, such as the crocheting and embroidery which were Lo's only artistic endeavors. But the jewelry making was a true profession mostly restricted to men, and Katherine dressed as a boy when she succeeded in getting her father to influence his professional neighbors to apprentice her.

She carved the intaglios and cameos, some of which she wore in later years, and fashioned and built their silver and gold settings with the foot-bellows operated gas torch and special hand-made tools of the trade. She remembered having to daily clean her fingernails into the barrel containing the dust swept from the floor, work tables, and benches, and how periodically the barrel contents, along with the artisan's smocks and work tables and benches, were burned in an incinerator designed to recover the gold and silver dust. She remembered the workers who painted the luminous dials on watches and who, with the ignorance of that time, pointed their brushes in their pursed lips without knowing they were ingesting a highly toxic substance that shortened their lives.

Katherine remembered her youthful apprenticeship fondly, and brought that enthusiasm and all those skills into the crafts she taught her children. Her love of metals was reflected in the gold and silver paints used lavishly in our craft projects, and the art of annealing base relief images in aluminum and copper foil.

A.J. inherited her love of metal and advanced it when she taught him the art of metalwork, beating out designs in heavier gauge aluminum and copper such as trays and boxes, as physical therapy to deal with the results of his elbow surgery at the age of seven.

He also tried soap sculpture, carving out rather rugged looking female torsos from the large orange colored bars of Octagon soap. And when Mary Isom taught us papier mache and ceramic fundamentals, he made a rakish looking devil's head and we all took a crack at imbedding glass mosaics in plaster of Paris, the glass obtained from the many different disposable colored bottles of the day.

I developed a love of jewelry and sensuous fabrics that made some fear for my gender identity, but it was only partly inherited from Katherine's love of jewelry and, moreso, the influence of the *Prince Valiant* comic strip and movies of the day where King Arthur's knights and pirates and Sabu all cavorted in velvet capes and bejeweled trappings while searching for treasures of precious jewels and gold coins.

When the books of our family library began to include volumes with large full color illustrations of the latest findings about ancient Egypt, A.J. developed a fascination for their mysticism and two dimensional artwork with little or no perspective. He began to trace drawings from the *Book of The Dead* and incorporate the designs and symbolism in his metal art, where before his designs were borrowed from the Vikings.

I found these family books fascinating, but was more enthralled with the new art magazine, *Coronet,* which always had several photographic picture stories with at least one devoted to erotic material or nudes. I began to clip and collect these photographs of nude statues and occasional live nudes, and Katherine wisely ignored my increased interest in 'art.'

My earliest efforts at serious art began around the age of eight, probably prompted by A.J.'s soap sculptures and Coronet Magazine, and were pencil, pen and ink, and water color renderings of goddess like nudes, sans areola and pubic hair, who surveyed the world from seashores or mountain tops. In the fourth and fifth grades, I published a hand illustrated hand printed one page class newspaper which filled out the lack of newsworthy events in the class with trivial information about nature and geography from our family library. When the war began, my classroom doodlings turned to aircraft and the rapid evolution of aircraft design with such classics as the sleek P47 fighter plane, the twin hulled P38, and the Flying Fortress bomber.

When I began to take an interest in movies, I became a cartoonist, illustrating the covers of school chum's notebooks with rapid sketches of the humanized animals that peopled the movie cartoons of the day. Around the age of ten, I wrote both Walt Disney and Leon Schlesinger (creator of *Looney Tunes* and *Merry Melodies)* to announce my intention of becoming a movie animator. To my dismay, I did not hear anything from my major hero, Walt Disney, but Leon Schleslinger sent a nice letter telling me to contact him again after I'd graduated from an art school.

Talented friends of the family, the paintings and etchings which adorned our walls, and the books of the family library were all factors that made most of us graphic oriented beings who wanted to capture all that we saw and liked in some form that we could keep with us forever.

This artistic expression expanded from its' two and three dimensional forms when the culture vultures of the Bay decided they wanted a 'Little Theater.' Le Petite Theatre in New Orleans had achieved national fame with its' professionalism, and more than a few of the more cultured and affluent residents of the Bay were concurrent or ex-patriot New Orleans residents. Adeline Knoblock, a syndicated columnist and author of the day (and the Bay's resident Jewish intellectual), was one of the promoters for a little theater. Another was Caroline Keifer whose private life was plagued with scandal, but whose strength and cultural interests brought her and Adeline to Katherine's door, Katherine being the town's resident 'artiste.'

They decided to produce a minstrel show to raise seed money to start the little theater. I was about thirteen and had developed an artistic profile in the community when they asked me to create a stage set for them with the magnificent budget of $13. I built a ten foot wide by eight foot high background centerpiece designed as a blackface with high hat, white gloves, and polka dot tie. The eyes, mouth, and reflection in the high hat were cut out of the mattress carton cardboard on 1"x2" framework and covered from the rear with white tissue paper so they could be back lighted. The red and blue polka dots on the tie were garishly glittered. The three flats on each of the side wings were lighted from the bottom with colored lights created by bending a white card into an orange crate as a reflector, mounting a wired socket with 150 watt bulb in the center, and stapling colored cellophane over the front as a filter.

The flats were painted with these alternate red and blue colored lights and wired so they could be switched to all red, all blue, or a combination. The overall effect was quite impressive, despite the fact that the local hardware dealer's wife couldn't figure out that we switched the lights from a distant location and stuck her hand through the cellophane to unscrew the bulbs during one performance.

The seed money went as the down payment on an old abandoned cotton gin building which became the home of the Bay St. Louis Little Theater which distinguished itself for decades with a high level of professionalism and as the cradle of notable careers and written works. Clay Blair, who had grown up in the Bay and was a longtime editor of *Saturday Evening Post* and author of *The Atomic Submarine,* premiered his first play there. Other original works and outstanding performers chose it to refine their product.

I continued to participate in the little theater, illustrating some of their programs, designing and building some of the stage sets, and sometimes in the capacity of stage manager. I built their first light dimmer board fabricated from ancient rheostats Mr. Zerr contributed, a 'sound effects' console consisting of a doorbell, a buzzer, and a telephone ringer, and I built, dressed, and lit sets for many a production.

My crowning achievement was building a fire effect for the climatic scene of *The Bad Seed* in which our twisted little anti-heroine burns her protagonist up in the off-stage garage. I mounted four photo-reflector bulbs with orange filters on a vertical stand and suspended in front of them a long grass skirt made of black Mylar and red cellophane hand cut strips stapled to a small horizontal board at the top which was suspended on each end by rubber bands. A string attached to this board animated the grass skirt as the dimmer on the orange lights was brought up while cellophane was slowly crushed within inches of a microphone to produce the sound of fire which was increased with the amplifier volume control. The effect was merely seen reflected on a flat and bush viewed through a window on the stage set, but I beamed with pride when some of the audience got up to flee, convinced the backstage was on fire.

The other artistic dimension that had always been in our home was music. Will Schmidt had put his hand to any musical instrument that came his way, and though he had passed away when I was born, his Martin guitar, custom made Italian mandolin, and left handed concertina were still around. Aunt Thelma's piano and Katherine's violin were, of course, the living testimony of inherent talent and love of music.

Katherine's violin found company in the Bay when Mrs. Goldman, the pianist at the Methodist Church, offered her home to a string quartet composed of Katherine, Rene deMoultlizen Jr., and Mr. Weston and his wife, Mrs. Goldman being the only one with a piano. The group did a variety of chamber music, folk music, and some of the heavier classics. They were good enough to have their own muchly appreciated, though unpaid, Sunday morning radio program which emanated from nearby Gulfport.

For a while the quartet added the talents of a 'musical whistler,' a butch looking lady named Bea whose talents as a whistler were truly professional. It was an interesting addition to a string quartet, and Bea was an interesting lady, at least to a child in his sub-teens who had never seen a lesbian before. Bea paid court to Katherine unsuccessfully, and eventually drifted away from the group.

Mrs. Goldman was another of those strong willed ladies in town. White haired for as long as I can remember, she raised three sons with the very infrequent help of the Commodore who, it seemed, was always away at sea. Of course, she had the help of Sandy, the large mongrel dog who yapped at the alligators who would approach their back yard which bordered a swamp and offered the lure of their chicken house; Inky and Cameo, the two cocker spaniels who had the run of the house; and Tchikowski, the large aged parrot the Commodore had brought home from his travels and who constantly finked on the cocker spaniels who weren't allowed on the furniture, "Bad dog, bad dog, get off the sofa, bad dog!!!"

Tchikowski was one of those animal phenomenons who had a *New Orleans Times Picayune* Sunday supplement feature article devoted to him when he was eventually donated to Audubon Park Zoo in New Orleans in later years. There were countless stories of his prodigious vocabulary and precocious use of it which convinced most, myself included, that he had some sense of human values and a somewhat mischievous sense of humor. He would mimic street vendors, "Strawwwwwwberries, strawwwwberries, get your fresh strawwwberries," then laugh as the Commodore ran out to the street with his pail looking for the vendor. He would flirt, "Hey, pretty baby, come gimme a kiss," but only with attractive younger women, and he'd spread his comb and do a little dance when they'd blow him a kiss.

Musically speaking, he understood pitch and key and he'd sing along with the string quartet as they rehearsed or, even more amazing, he'd sing an obbligato he'd create himself, but always in the proper key and in harmony. And he delighted in music, not wanting the rehearsal to end, "Come on, let's do it again, from the top now," and he'd trail off on one of his own melodious creations.

I was an ardent admirer of music, reputed to have shaken my foot or my fanny whenever music was around ever since I was in diapers. Certainly I was an admirer of musicians, principally my mother. However, it wasn't until I was nine and the school prompted me to take up drum that I became a participant. Being self employed and, from my perspective at the time, affluent, I was proud to invest $25 in the gold sparkling marching drum that was slightly less than half my size. I don't recall any particular accomplishment or thrill involved in my 'drum experience,' although, intermittently through the years, I did at times own and play drums, but usually in the context of creating an ensemble or recording multiple tracks.

The piano entered my life through a quirk of fate. About the age of ten, I heard a terrible sound coming from across the street one morning. I investigated to find the Sellier children using hammers to pound on the keyboard of an old upright piano in their front yard. When I asked why they were hitting the keyboard like that, they replied, "To see the ivories fly in the air." I begged them to stop and they replied, "Why should we."

Without any prior thought on the subject, and probably, for no other reason than to save the piano, I said, "Because I want to buy the piano. How much do you want for it?" After consulting with their mother, we agreed on the price of $25, provided they move it into my living room, complete with all the damaged ivories they could find on the surrounding ground.

Now I was the proud owner of a somewhat damaged old upright piano, although I thought of it more as one of the disabled birds we'd sometimes find in the yard and put into bandages and splints to heal before releasing once again to freedom. But this piano would not fly away on its own, and the logical alternative was for me to learn how to help it fulfill its destiny.

Katherine inquired around and found my first teacher, Natalie Pienas, cousin to Rosalie and her mother. Natalie lived about ten blocks away, was a dark wiry black lady a little one side or the other of forty, and was perhaps a little bit crazy. She started me out at fifty cents a lesson twice a week with a militantly strict disciplinary attitude which progressed, over the next three months, into frightening intimidation replete with a ruler to the knuckles and crazed screaming at each and every mistake.

A little further investigation turned up Mrs. Weber, a slightly more mature German country lady who lived with her stout sister and both of whom taught at St. Agnes Academy, the parochial girl's school near their house. Mrs. Weber, with her dyed blonde hair, and her sister, with her dyed black hair, were comfortable easy-going ladies with infinite patience and the wisdom to concentrate on the love of music as well as the technique of performance. She would always include a little of the history of Beethoven, Brahms, Lizt, or Mozart, even if her knowledge of that period of history and the eccentricity of some of the Masters was a little naive, or possibly just censored. To illustrate some things, she would perform in a rolling romping style that somehow made everything sound like a waltz at a barn dance, but she could tell what a student needed to know, and she could hear the 'touch' and 'style' that I evoked from the keyboard, and she took note.

After a year or two of lessons, I came to be known as a local prodigy and was called upon to perform for public events. Where before Katherine had, for want of a baby sitter, taken me into dirt floor churches and gold plated synagogues and cathedrals to hear her play the violin, now I was called into these temples of worship to play the classics whose composers had been commissioned by the church to create, the church being the principal patron of the arts then and the principal medium for their presentation now.

There were other mediums, though, and I remember playing for an elementary school graduation in the rural town of Lakeshore which had never had music at their graduation ceremonies before. They didn't have a room big enough at the school, so it was held at a recreation center which had only screen on the windows and, as they unloaded an old upright piano from a battered pickup truck, I could tell the instrument was in shambles. I discovered half the keys didn't function and I had to literally pound the keyboard to get any sound whatsoever from those that did. Nonetheless, as I beat out *Pomp And Circumstance,* the audience sat enthralled. I was so embarrassed I wanted to cry, but, afterward, I was deluged with sincere compliments from people who had never heard classical music before and never traveled more than a few miles from their home or owned a radio.

The radio programs of the day did offer fine music. There was the *Longine Whitnauer Hour* with symphonic performances by leading artists of the day. My favorite, however, was *The Alec Templeton Show,* and I had been a fan for more than a year before I learned that classical pianist Templeton was blind. He made music a joyous thing, and he de-mystified the classics. His greatest trick was to have people in the audience call out five notes at random, then compose a piece using those five notes in the sequence they were called out as the theme, then to do variations on the theme until he had composed a mini-concerto, and he did this routine on each and every show. This routine sparked my efforts to compose much earlier than I would have attempted otherwise.

Composing began after the first six months of

lessons, as soon as I comprehended the rudiments of written music and developed enough facility at the keyboard to enjoy the dynamics of shading and syncopation. Katherine had just returned from surgery at Keesler field, her marriage to Francis Wilson providing the medical attention afforded a military dependent and which she desperately needed through the years for her 'female problems.' For her homecoming, I composed my first instrumental number which I titled *Gypsy* simply because its syncopation made me think of a dancing gypsy girl. Its 32 bars were traditionally formatted, but it was constructed around chord changes I gravitated to by instinct or by ear, because I couldn't have understood them academically until years after I finished any formal musical training. Katherine was weak and wan, but sweetly appreciative of my musical gesture.

I continued to write brief instrumental numbers, mostly elaborations of five finger exercises or imitations of the masters such as Bach's busyness or Beethoven's somberness. Then, about the time I noticed girls, I began to write song lyrics to my music, and, later, music to my poetry. Where before, playing the classics had given me a voice for my emotions, pounding out Lizt's *Hungarian Rhapsody No. 2* when I was angry or frustrated and frolicking through Strauss when I was exuberant, now composing words and music gave me a direct literal expression for my feelings. Many years later I wrote a song that truly expressed my attitude toward music. Titled *Language Of The Soul,* the lyrics went like this:

> *Music is the language of the soul*
> *It transcends the sands of time*
> *Survives from the days of old*
> *Tells us of the thoughts of man*
> *The secrets his heart holds*
> *Yes music is the language...*
>   *the language of the soul.*

More lasting than products of man's hands
More reaching than treks to distant lands
More true than these stumbling words I sing
Is the feeling—the feeling music brings.

I eventually exhausted what Mrs. Weber could teach me, and I moved on to Mrs. Smith, the music teacher at the public school who only took exceptional private students. Mrs. Smith was slightly younger, had red hair, and drove a little Austin Midget that fascinated me. She was very strict and challenging to me, hoping to groom me as the school's first entrant in the state piano competitions. The required composition that year was both challenging and uninspiring with little or no room for schmaltzy emoting, which was my forte. Instead, it called for a refinement of technique which I had not achieved with Mrs. Weber, but which Mrs. Smith brought me up to, not without more than a little stress on my part.

At the state competition I walked away from my peers at the preliminaries, but, just before the finals that evening, I met my closest competitor, a beautiful girl who asked if I would let her go on first as she was nervous. Naturally I acquiesced and she did a fair job that would still not have beat my morning performance. When I went on, she moved into the wings where I could see her and smiled at me continuously. I started Beethoven's *Contra Dance,* but found myself thinking of her. Halfway through the number, I completely forgot where I was, paused, resumed at the wrong place, and came in second. As I walked offstage to modest applause, I could see Mrs. Smith glaring at me from the front row, and I was so embarrassed I didn't even go pick up my silver medal.

I had the offer of becoming the 'protege' of an elderly retired concert pianist. This lady was from Uruguay and her beach home, which we had visited during several community fundraisers, was beautifully appointed with heavy South American furniture handmade of rare woods, and wall hangings and trays exquisitely decorated with exotic butterflies and moths. She rarely played the ornate grand piano in her large living room, but displayed the evidence of her former prominence on those rare occasions when she, sometimes in concert with Katherine, contributed her musical talents to community functions.

This lady did not normally take piano students and certainly did not need to do so for an income, so her offer to 'sponsor' me gratis was extremely flattering. That is, until Katherine heard through the underground that this mature woman was notorious for seducing young boys, whereupon the wrinkles in her face together with excessive makeup and eccentric costuming made her suddenly appear jaded. Katherine declined the concert artist's invitation without even consulting me.

Katherine sat me down one day for a serious talk, and asked me how I felt about the public school I attended. She knew I had trouble with the bullies in class who were set back so many grades they were three and four years older than the rest of us. Being the precocious and talented kid in class meant I was the target for their frustrations and abuse. The academic standards of the school were extremely poor, the Superintendent having concentrated on sports and being suspect of related sports gambling activities.

Katherine told me I had been offered a scholarship to the local Catholic parochial school, St. Stanislaus. They had an extensive boarding facility as well as local enrollment, superior academic credentials and standards, and the best swimming pier in town. Only years later did she tell me that the offer came from a high-ranking nun at St. Agnes Academy who had noticed me at Mrs. Weber's piano recitals conducted at St. Agnes' auditorium. The only catch was that I was expected to become a Catholic. I declined.

My blossoming as a prodigy also prompted my Godfather, H. Grady Meador, to reassert his interest in adopting me. I was summoned to Grady and Sadie's home to have 'high tea' with Sadie. I was dressed in my one and only suit, instructed to be on my best behavior, and delivered to face Aunt Sadie all alone. I held the teacup with appropriately raised little finger, ate the dainty cucumber sandwiches without spilling anything, and performed Beethoven's *Moonlight Sonata* on their rarely used Steinway piano like a trained seal. The conversation revolved around whether I would be interested in seeing Europe, attending a good boarding school, and learning to address Grady and Sadie as 'father' and 'mother.' The clincher was when she emphasized how severely restricted my contact with Katherine and the family would be.

The truth was, Sadie had already picked Grady's successor, her nephew who, like Sadie had, acquired a new middle name to become D. Boone Pickens. In later years he ruled the remnants of Gulf Oil Company, subsequently known as Mesa Petroleum, and thought of as a controversial exponent of the art of corporate raiding and takeovers. Perhaps he was the best choice, but who knows how I might have developed under Grady's tutelage and what good things might have been done with all that money and power. Of course, I might have ended up murdering Aunt Sadie, too.

Long after Grady and Sadie had passed away and it would not offend him, and as a professional expedient much as the adoption of a middle name was to Sadie and her nephew, I changed my middle name from Grady to Karl because, at that point in my life, my compatriots in the film industry believed that Germans were the best cinematographers. I was of German descent, but it was not reflected in my name sufficiently, and Karl with a "K" seemed to do the trick. I have come to answer to the name Karl so much that I have to relearn how to respond to Bill or William.

In high school, I began to make money with my piano by forming trios or quartets to play 'casuals' or 'one night gigs.' My principal sidekick was a country boy named Billy Ray who played trombone, an unlikely instrument for a trio or quartet, but Billy Ray owned the car or, at least, his father did.

Billy Ray's father was a blind piano tuner who lived in Logtown along Pearl River, the state line between Mississippi and Louisiana. The white bearded old man stayed in their ramshackle old house, which bore not the least trace of its original paint, constantly rebuilding the same piano over and over and never finishing it. Billy Ray's short rotund mother was a waitress at the White Kitchen, a Highway 90 eatery halfway between Bay St. Louis and New Orleans.

The car in question was an ancient square shaped Chevrolet that must have pre-dated the 1930's. We had to start it with a hand crank that could break your arm if you didn't disengage it fast enough once it started, which was never as swiftly as you'd like. The car broke down more than half the time and we would pray that it would behave on the way to the job, even if it had to break down on the way home, which always occurred in the middle of nowhere.

Our gigs were at 'roadhouses' such as Boscoe's in Slidell, Louisiana, and similar out of the way places where a raw unpolished group could risk refining their act without the audience or management realizing they were less than thoroughly professional. We made $15 or $20 a night for the group, about $4 to $8 apiece, out of which we were constantly pouring gas and parts into the decrepit car.

Concurrent with my developing musical interests, my job in Mr. Zerr's projection booth and growing collection of slides and educational filmstrips led me in logical order to an interest in photography. My stepfather, Francis Wilson, enjoyed photography as a hobby and, though he no longer had the equipment he had left and lost in his former home in Detroit, he still brought home photography magazines that began my education in the subject.

I started using Katherine's folding Kodak that delivered eight 2 1/4"x3 1/4" negatives per roll. A simple camera with limited controls, I nonetheless learned the principals upon which it functioned and deduced that I could take time exposures with it, and even closeups if I taped onion skin paper in the film plane to provide a crude 'focusing ground glass' and extended the bellows beyond the limited increments on its focusing bed before I loaded the camera.

When Adeline Knoblock wanted A.J. to repair a meerschaum pipe carved in the likeness of Leda And The Swan, one item from her extensive art collection gathered in her world travels, I took the opportunity of photographing the tantalizing piece of erotica in closeup using these techniques. I also learned to adapt it to A.J.'s microscope and make microphotographs of my own hair with all its questionable bumps and scales.

Francis' magazines led me to believe I needed a 35mm camera, but the only one I could afford at the time was a simple Spartus 35mm camera with fixed focus lens. While it wasn't even as versatile as the larger folding camera, it was much handier for candids and allowed me to shoot slide film which I could project in my slide projector. Some of the first color I shot with it was of Tarzan Oaks at sunrise. I quickly progressed to photographing bathing beauties at the beach. The message in the ads of the photo magazines was not lost on me.

About the time I started high school, the new school bandleader rented our next door cottage. Mr. Wembly and his attractive young wife were from one of the great lakes states, and he was a kind man and a good teacher. Even though I wasn't one of his music students, despite his efforts to recruit me, he shared his knowledge of photography with me and generously allowed me to use an old Exacta 127 single lens reflex camera he had brought back from Germany after his military duty in World War II. This sophisticated camera taught me the virtues of a professional instrument and I started using it to provide photos along with the artwork illustrations I executed for the school paper.

Later in high school, I learned that our school had never had a school annual because of the cost of photography, and the type of equipment needed to capture things like sports action and super sharp people pictures called for truly professional equipment. In those days, that meant a 'press camera,' the large format cameras which accepted a variety of film mediums, interchangeable lenses, and sophisticated accessories.

By this time, my interest in photography had led me to work at Bennett's Photo Lab in New Orleans during the summer, and, eventually, I saved enough money to buy my first press camera at Bennett's Photo Store; a 2 1/4"x3 1/4" Model C Busch Pressman with all the trimmings. With it I illustrated subsequent editions of my school's annuals during my high school years. I was thirteen at the time, but almost six feet tall and as confident of my talents as most adult professionals.

The first summer I had my press camera, I was staying with Lo in New Orleans in order to work in the photo lab. One night Audubon Park's riding stables caught fire and I ran the block from Lo's apartment house to the stables to take my first news photos of the terrified horses running out of the burning buildings. I had the presence of mind to call the night editor at the Time Picayune and they asked me to come down to their darkroom where they processed and bought my pictures for $50, the largest amount of money I had ever seen for a single nights work.

Photography became an extension of the graphic arts for me, a different technology, but still a fine art if it were so motivated. I knew that someday somehow I'd be able to pull all these talents together; the moralistic plays I wrote for our marionette shows, the music and lyrics I composed at the keyboard, the drawings and stage crafts and photography which somehow was all intended to achieve a common end, to freeze in time that which is good and beautiful and worthy. It took me another decade and the company of more experienced and greatly talented friends to have the courage to dare to apply all these talents to film production.

This page: *(top)* the author as an 8-year-old drummer, *(center)* as a 13-year-old pianist, and, *(bottom)* as a 15-year-old photographer.

Right page: *(top)* Will Schmidt's 1913 Patton Street Gazette designed to entertain his two daughters at boarding school; *(bottom)* the author as a 13-year-old photographer, captures Audubon Park Stables on fire and makes first professional newspaper sale.

The Patton Street Gazette

Mr. Phlipp Pelican on the weather

Great Excitement in Mexico - U.S. Army Victorious. Mexicans routed by Strategy of Celestial.

Scientists & Geologists Puzzled

School Board asks paltry sum to repair the school room

Terrible Accident on Canal Street

Amusements

Chapter Ten
MY PEERS

Throughout my life, my personal and professional peers were not necessarily my chronological peers. Friends and lovers, collaborators and co-workers were, for the most part, a decade or a generation my senior. Among the chronological peers of my early school years, few were friends and none were lovers, collaborators, or co-workers.

In elementary school I played with the neighborhood children out of desperation, but found the company of girls more to my liking than the aggressiveness and limited interests of boys. With the affluence I acquired by earning my own pocket money after the age of eight, I bought acceptance from the boys by sharing my collection of comic books, *Big-Little* books (semi-soft cover literature for children), and a collection of cap pistols which were essential to playing 'cowboys and Indians.' But my growing attitude that movie cowboys should not have the license to kill Indians indiscriminately, as they did in movies of the day, led to my eventual exclusion from the macho circle of pre-adolescent neighborhood boys.

My affinity for girls made my manhood questionable, my talents made me the target of jealousy, and my fair complected pudgy body made me the scapegoat of bullies. For the most part I adapted comfortably to the role of outcast, did not contest the accusations of being an intellectual snob, and, in my high school years, was amused at the suspicions of being gay.

By the time I entered high school, my body had slimmed down to an impressive physique, my acne had subsided into a manageable inconvenience, and I had learned how to train a wave in my corn silk straight blonde hair that mimicked the wave in Katherine's hair.

The bullies no longer picked on me, the girls started to cater to my performing talents as a photographer and pianist, and the pecking order of adolescents made a place for me somewhere near the top despite my relative poverty and past ostracization.

There were three chronological categories of male classmates at that time: the returning servicemen five and more years past the norm who were resuming their high school education with little or no social contact with their younger classmates, the academic incompetents two to five years past the norm who had failed and been set back several grades and were as clumsy at socializing as they were at their lessons, and the rest of us who were more or less the normal age for our school grade.

There were three boys who survived the four years of high school in the same class with me. Although I had passed up most of the bullies who had plagued me in elementary school by skipping them several grades, one of these three was the biggest bully of the entire school who had been set back enough grades to be in my class through most of high school.

He might have been handsomer, and possibly brighter, if back street brawling and high school athletics had not scarred his face and his whole concept of relating to his peers. Like many of the top high school athletes, his edge was actually being several years more physically mature than most of his opponents in whatever sport he attempted, an edge which the sports minded principal at that time was suspected of deliberately creating in order to benefit the high school gambling interests in which he was involved. These athletes were guaranteed passing grades and given monetary and other inducements to secure their sports participation. Although this young man harassed me the first year of high school, he eventually backed off. Perhaps he acquired some respect for my occasional efforts to stand up to him, but most likely he simply found it politically expedient, or perhaps it was through the intercession of a woman who I later discovered was this boy's father's mistress and a friend of my mother.

The other two boys were the two handsomest boys in the class, I sometimes coming in a close third as years progressed. Martin Noto was the brainiest of the two, trying nobly to live up to the ambitions his adoring mother had for him. He was six months younger than me and had a trim physique, smooth olive complexion, black curly hair, and a classic Roman profile.

His mother kept him dressed immaculately and indulged him in whatever props would aid him socially from the first ball point pen ever seen in our school (it would write under water) to the gold religious medals that hung on gold chains around his neck. Despite being spoiled and prone to tantrums in dealing with his mother, at school Martin was quiet, studious, and won his popularity by being agreeable and a joiner.

He was usually a class officer of some kind, worked on the school paper and yearbook, was a member of the debating team, and participated in most sports, barely missing out on a boxing scholarship because of his young age, but succeeding in getting into college nonetheless. His family lived a working class existence on his father's earnings as a butcher at the principal grocery in the heart of town, and a week-end night job calling out Bingo numbers at one of the beach front night clubs. After the 1947 hurricane, Federal assistance poured into the devastated area, and people who had never had anything before were suddenly provided brand new housing free or with low interest or no interest loans and the promise that most of the loan would be excused in a few short years.

Suddenly Martin's family had a brand new house completely furnished with the newest of everything right down to a washing machine and fancy new kitchen appliances. The living room had a console radio that picked up short wave bands and had a green 'magic tuning eye' in the center. The large bookshelves were filled with brand new books bought solely upon the advice of the bookstore owner and none of which his parents had ever read. The new living room set had plastic covers that never came off unless his mother was entertaining in her eternal efforts to 'rise' in society.

A pretty lady with a good figure becoming prematurely matronly, Martin's mother had a passion to better herself and her son's options in life. She joined every civic association that would have her and campaigned for every office within them that might afford her name in print. She had attended business school, but still managed to murder the King's English and was mercifully oblivious of the faux pas she committed as she attempted to mimic the social graces to which she aspired.

She considered me a good influence on Martin and promoted our friendship with good food from her kitchen and frequent invitations to her home and social events. She solicited my advice as to which books on her living room shelves Martin should read, and which of my mother's friends might need and accept her participation in their civic projects. Martin was sometimes embarrassed by her aggressiveness, but, reflecting on my own familial relations, I admired her loyalty and devotion to her son and defended her when others would deride her malapropisms and misconceptions, such as thinking Madame Butterfly was a fictional insect like Jiminey Cricket.

My mother tried to reciprocate Mrs. Noto's hospitality by forming 'The Revelers,' a teen group she created to keep us out of trouble and consisting mostly of Martin, Odelle, myself, and any girls we could lure into the fold. Her format was cross between craft classes and a book review club, with board and word games to fill the gaps. The refreshments in our home were minimal, snow balls in the summer and popcorn in the winter, but my peers seemed to like it.

I now recognize that Katherine continued this process in later years when her children had left home and she became the town librarian. She expanded the libraries programs to include different age levels of children, the involvement of arts and crafts in those programs, and the inclusion of the black children of St. Rose deLima parochial school, her first step in integrating the library..

Odelle Saucier was a contrast to Martin in that he was extremely fair with blonde hair, and in his total disinterest in improving his mind. He was ten months older than I, had a trim figure, and looked much like a boyish Robert Redford, although in those days he probably compared himself to Ronald Coleman. Odelle was a true Narcissist. He spent more time looking at himself in a mirror, combing his hair, and taking baths than any man I've ever known. He once sought my advice about skin rashes, thinking he had caught a venereal disease by kissing girls, only to find they came from bathing too much. Like Martin, he was a dapper dresser, participated in sports, and ran for class office every year. Popularity was an all-consuming goal in Odelle's life, and yet, as much as he wanted to be known as a ladies man, he fulfilled very few of the romantic opportunities it afforded.

Odelle's family was of Scotch, Irish, and French descent, and of the same working class as Martin's, elevated after the 1947 hurricane to what passed for middle class in Bay St. Louis. Either his family was clannish, or Odelle was for some reason uncomfortable around them and always managed to avoid Martin or I ever meeting them or entering his house. I remember seeing his mother only once, a thin attractive dishwater blonde with a harried face old beyond her years. In that brief moment of exposure, she seemed proud and solicitous of Odelle, but he seemed embarrassed to introduce her to us.

Martin, Odelle, and I met in the eighth grade and buddied together through most of high school. We formed what we considered an invincible trio for being teacher's pets, wooing the girls, and maintaining a wide margin of upmanship between ourselves and all the other males in the class. We acted as a mutual support group when faced with the reality that our parochial school competition had all the money, the cars, and the principal girls we lusted after all through high school.

Actually, none of the boys in our school had cars, except for a few returned veterans in their twenties, and that's partly why the cream of the girl crop often had parochial school beaus. I had very little to do with the girls of my high school acquaintance. While I had preferred the company of girls in my elementary school years, in my high school years I preferred the company of the adult women I worked with in my summer jobs or the friends of Katherine who treated me as a professional and involved me in civic projects such as The Little Theater. High school girls, while many were pretty and tempting, seemed shallow and vacuous.

That did not keep me from occasionally having crushes on them, which I rarely acted upon. Around the third or fourth grade there was a girl named Betty Cook with a tall trim figure, long blonde hair, and almost oriental eyes. I bought a garish ring at the dime store and, one day at recess, slipped the ring on her finger and a kiss on her cheek. She wiped her cheek in disgust and threw the ring in the bushes, which effectively kept me a considerable distance from her until her family moved away.

Somewhere around the sixth or seventh grade, another Betty with curly blonde hair, a great tan, and nouveau riche parents who considered me good company for her, caught my fancy. This Betty had toys like a brand new baby grand piano, two riding horses in the stables out back, and a surrey with a fringe on the top for rides in the country.

She fancied the class jock, the handsome but less than bright son of a fisherman, whom she introduced to the joys of sexuality at a very early age. Encouraged by her parents to keep my company, she considered honoring me with her favors. That is, until one day when the two of us were horsing around in the hayloft and all her advances went unnoticed by me. As we sat on the steps leading to the hayloft, we saw the rooster copulating with the hens. Betty suggested we could do that, and I confessed I didn't know what they were doing. That was the last day she pretended to satisfy her parents desire that she associate with me.

A third Betty was my early high school crush. Betty Lusk had long blonde wavy hair, an angelic face, and a perfect figure mature beyond her years. She was by far the most beautiful and the most sought after girl in school, and, if perfect grades were any measure, perhaps the most intelligent. She lived around the corner on Carol Avenue and, as freshman and sophomore classmates, we saw a lot of each other. The day I got my courage up enough to invite her to the movies, her mother informed me she was out sailing with one of the richest boys in town several years her senior, and I detected a note of pity in her mother's voice which convinced me not to try again.

I don't think I had a fixation on blonde-haired Bettys. I was enamored of Cherie Green whose red hair, freckled fair skin, gentle features, and womanly figure seemed appropriate to an old English setting in Scotland. I won a dance contest with shapely brown haired Ruth Carver. And Irma Joan Lee's drum majorette figure vied for my attention along with the Baldwin Acrosonic spinet piano her family acquired after the 1947 hurricane. But none of these attachments resulted in 'going steady,' as high school relationships were referred to in those days.

In my sophomore year I bought a portable phonograph, having tired of the low fidelity of the old acoustical Victrola in the living room, and having visions of 'beach parties' where a portable phonograph was an ideal inducement to lure the girls. It was a Sears product with a metal luggage style housing, a wind-up spring motor that only played 78 rpm records, and relatively 'hi-fidelity' tube electronics powered by a heavy 45 volt dry cell that was so expensive I only used the thing a few brief weeks each summer. All I had were scratchy second-hand 78's of Billie Holiday, Glenn Miller, and Louis Armstrong, but that was sufficient to set the scene.

Martin, Odelle, and I would take the girls swimming in the moonlight, teasing them by putting the florescent multicolored jellyfish in their hair like a crown of jewels in the night, and hoping to find an excuse for the accidental contact of our bodies on the slick smooth wet skin of our teenage dates. I did all right with the swimming, the disc jockeying, and the roasting of hot dogs and marshmallows over the fire, but, when the blankets were spread and the light of the fire started to die out, I was at a loss.

Odelle was always the first to start 'smooching,' as petting was called then, and Martin always followed a self conscious second. My date and I would watch the two couples fully clothed bodies squirming in the dark on the blankets, hearing the sound effects of osculation and Martin's girl occasionally having to tell him what to do, while Odelle's girl sometimes had to tell him what not to do.

Sometimes my date was as timid as I was and happy to settle for a walk along the water's edge, hand in hand, and, if I felt really brave, perhaps a few chaste kisses standing up or leaning against a tree. If she was more sophisticated, however, she would feel insulted by my lack of aggressiveness and find fault with me and,

God forbid, any belated advances I made to appease her. Little wonder I never took the same girl to the beach more than once.

The beginning of my junior year with my peers in Bay St. Louis was interrupted by a change in Katherine's plans after Lola died. Lo had willed her two remaining pieces of real estate to her two daughters; the Prytania Street wood frame three unit apartment house to Aunt Thelma, and the Patton Street wood frame four unit apartment house to Katherine, as Katherine had dependents and greater need for the possible added income. Katherine decided to move to New Orleans to better manage her only source of income.

She also decided to sell the Bay St. Louis cottage to finance repairs on the New Orleans apartment house, fearful of renting the cottage as an absentee landlord and all the memories of unseen damage done by tenants and rents uncollected from afar. I begged her to sell the apartment house rather than the Bay property, doubting her ability to manage the aging apartment house and seeing the capital best invested in an interest paying account. I also felt she would be better emotionally supported by her friends and lifestyle in the Bay, as would I by my high school peers.

At fourteen I had reached my full height of 5'11." I looked like an adult, I talked like an adult, and sometimes I even thought like an adult, but without the experience of an adult. Although my projection was ultimately correct, I had not tempered it with consideration of Katherine's pride in being able to manage the apartment house. She sold the Bay cottage and we moved to New Orleans.

Only after we had been in the apartment house for some months did I realize another motive Katherine had for making the move. A.J. lived in the upper rear apartment which he had decorated with his metal art, various cutlasses in heraldic arrangements, and framed etchings, lithographs, and prints of esoterica from the family collections. Occasionally there would appear on the walls the original artwork of science fiction magazine or book covers which could be purchased through the mails via ads in the back of the science fiction pulp magazines of the day. These were usually macabre and sometimes erotic with such themes as the upper torso of a voluptuous woman attached to the body of a serpent as she held miniature versions of Flash Gordon and Buck Rogers in her long fingernailed hands, the obvious hunger on her face equally interpreted as cannibalism or sexual passion.

    A.J. worked as a draftsman at an industrial firm along the river, and his young male friends were followers of his guru like character and trappings, sometimes forming early chapters of Dianetics and other cults of the time. A.J.'s love life seemed non-existent. He admired some young women his age from afar, such as Father Carre's niece who sang in the choir at St. Patrick's cathedral, and the daughters of some of Katherine's friends. But his longstanding love had been Mary Isom, the talented artist his mother's age who now lived in Aunt Thelma's apartment house on Prytania Street. A.J. paid court to Mary and won an awkward and tenuous claim to her heart, and I suspect her body, which lasted for several years.

    Katherine viewed A.J.'s lifestyle with tolerant concern, rationalizing every non-conformity except the one she initially denied, but ultimately could not ignore. At the tender age of twenty-two, A.J. was an alcoholic. Integral with the moody decor of his apartment were the sight and smell of heavy sweet wine which no amount of cigar or pipe smoke could mask. Port and Muscatel, watered down in a decanter, drunk from various crystal and copper goblets, and accompanied by dried fruit and ginger snaps, were the eternal props of his romantic image and his body chemistry.

I was once again consigned to a portion of the kitchen in the large downstairs apartment with folding screens for my privacy. My contact with A.J. mostly centered around being a constant loser at chess while he continuously poured himself wine from a decanter at the marble inlaid round chess table in his apartment. At times he would attempt to teach me knife throwing, a skill he acquired as therapy for his elbows and wrists and with which he won competitions, splitting kitchen matches at ten paces ten times and more in a row. I was proudest of him when I'd be allowed to attend his performance in competitions at the fencing academies in the French Quarter where he was considered a master with the saber and epee. His backward turning wrists made him look awkward when drinking from a teacup, but gave him an unexpected edge when wielding a cutlass.

But A.J. lived in a bygone era compared to my chronological peers at Fortier High School, the first and last all male school I ever attended. My guide to survival there was Bill Newcomb, the boy across the street who was a year or two older and into rebuilding cars and driving his mother crazy with his hyperactive mischief. Bill protected me at school and in exchange expected me to be a follower in his misadventures from driving cars along the levee of the Mississippi River with all its' dangerous labyrinth of quicksand pools, to sodding his backyard with squares cut from the first tee of the Audubon Park golf course in the shape of his initials during the dark of night.

Bill was an extrovert, a male chauvinist, and an alleged ladies man, but I literally had to sit down and diagram a woman's genitals with pencil and paper to aid his clumsy efforts to play 'stinky-finger' with the one and only girl he ever dated, a lovely girl who ultimately married him and bore his children. His efforts to socially exploit my talents as a pianist succeeded in widening my circle of acquaintances, but failed in his eyes as I was not mature enough to fulfill the many romantic opportunities it provided.

This circle of teenagers centered around the hospitality of the Wakefield's whose teenage daughter needed every assistance to overcome her looks and lackluster personality. They lived on one side of a middle class duplex and, like their daughter, were a short pudgy couple, he with white hair and a dead end job in industry, she with no interests but to follow his lead. I played their ill-tuned upright piano for sing-alongs, ate the eternal snacks Mrs. Wakefield generously provided the gang, and humored Mr. Wakefield in his desire to co-author pop songs with me; he providing a title and me providing everything else.

The Wakefield's had an older son who came home from the service and bought one of the first 'modern' postwar automobiles produced, a 1949 Ford which dazzled us with its advanced styling. The son was six or seven-years-older than most of us, and he had a friend his own age who we addressed by his last name, Prunty.

Prunty was one of those men who feel more comfortable with a younger group than with their contemporaries. To us he was a mature leader who lived adventures we only dreamed of. He owned his own car, drank to excess regularly, and frequented the black brothels in wicked parts of the city. He would sit silently at the Wakefield's and refrain from participating in games or songs or camaraderie. But when the evening broke up, he'd take some of us boys to a bar, feed us beer, and constantly beat us at pinball games, all for the pleasure of being called a jolly good fellow and a pinball champion.

A tall thin man of average looks, I think Prunty felt very insecure around women. His counseling to us boys regarding women was worse than male chauvinism, it was the bankrupt sexuality of a 'Studs Lonigan.' We never saw him socially linked with a woman, and the women he'd introduce us to as 'easy prey' for us to practice on were slatternly and, though our age, more sexually mature than we could handle.

One night I mentioned I was going to see an attractive girl I had been hoping to seduce, my virginity having been a constant source of sport among the group. Prunty offered to chauffeur us to and from the movie and, to my surprise offered us beer and a drive through Audubon Park on the way home. The girl became drunk and allowed me to indulge in foreplay to the extent of fondling her breasts and masturbating her through her panties in the back seat of Prunty's parked car, while he silently smoked a cigarette nearby in the park. Though she resisted further advances, she would conveniently swoon at that point, providing an opportunity Prunty later referred to as "the old come and get it routine." I finally asked Prunty to drive us home without attempting anything further with the girl. I wondered if Prunty intended to have sex with the girl had I succeeded in seducing her, and thereafter I declined his periodic invitations to bars and three sided dates.

Life on Patton Street did not change too dramatically since I had lived there with Lo. Aunt Thelma continued to live in the other side of the downstairs apartment, what had been Lo's apartment before she passed away. I presume she and A.J. paid Katherine rent, but, after my resistance to the New Orleans move, Katherine did not make me privy to her business arrangements.

Aunt Thelma bought a small 20'x20' government surplus building, the kind with a screened upper section, no windows, and only one door, and she moved it up to the Hamburg property within sight of Jesse James cabin so she could stay in it while developing the land. She bought a 4-wheel drive jeep and attachments for it to farm the land, but all she ever accomplished was to build a sizable fish pond on the property we eventually gave to Jesse. She vacilated back and forth between Hamburg and Patton Street, her apartment with its beautiful grand piano locked away from me most of the time.

Katherine's life became stagnant. Her mother's friends had mostly passed away, her own New Orleans friends were scattered to the four winds. Her only occupations were the constant repairs to the old wood frame apartment house, which A.J. and I were ineffectual in accomplishing, and trying to modify A.J.'s drinking, although the only benefit she accomplished was helping him climb the stairs to his apartment without breaking any bones when he'd come home sloshed.

Finally, an electrical fire forced her to face the no-win position she was in with the aging structure. She committed herself to enough indebtedness to make the needed repairs and buy back the Bay cottage for twice what she had sold it for the previous year. One of the new doctors in town had bought it for $2500, claimed to have made repairs which were not evident and couldn't have cost more than a few hundred if they were, and demanded $5000 even though it was a depressed market, because he could see how desperate Katherine was to return to her former life.

Katherine also committed herself to maintaining the apartment house several more years until the debt was paid, with A.J. now moved downstairs to our old apartment so he wouldn't break his neck on the staircase and so his upstairs apartment could bring in more income.

During the summer before my senior year in high school, I made a new friend in Bay St. Louis. Dick was about a year older than me and would have been my senior classmate had his family not moved away before school began. A tall fellow of medium build, he made up for his only passable looks by being a 'hail fellow well met' kind of extrovert. Having come from somewhere in the interior of the state, he took pride in being a 'country boy' and was so solicitous of adults and 'good folk' like my mother, that Katherine found his ingratiating behavior a bit too much to bear. His family were protestant fundamentalists and his speech was sometimes peppered with references from 'the good book' and a firm belief in 'the will of God.'

Dick had glommed onto me at some civic event in which I was involved, and I welcomed his flattery and camaraderie after a years separation from my former high school chums in the Bay. The friendship was short lived because of his family's moving, but it was notable because of one brief incident which caused it to evaporate almost overnight.

St. Augustine's Seminary was created in 1923 as the first, and for many years only, school in North America for Negro students entering the priesthood. It was integrated years before the Supreme Court's ruling on integration, but, during my youth, St. Augustine's students were all black and were treated with respect by the town folk who pointed to the seminary with pride.

One day Dick and I were headed for my house on the narrow sidewalks of Second Street where two black seminary students were coming towards us, their black frocks and beaded rosaries swaying as they engaged in conversation. I moved to one side and ahead a bit, expecting Dick to fall in behind me to make way for the seminary students who veered to one side of the walk to make room for us also. To my surprise, Dick stepped forward beside me, puffed out his chest, and stretched out his elbows, forcing the seminary students to step off the sidewalk into the dirt. They gave him a dirty look as they passed and Dick glared at them in challenge, saying loudly to me, but mostly for their ears, "I can't stand these black bucks thinking they own the world just because someone gave them a uniform."

I had heard such remarks from a rare few children, teens, and adults before, but never from those I had chosen to associate with. My teen peers might use a derogatory racial term or tell a racial joke in the private company of other teen males, but never before a female or an adult, and never never in the presence of a black who might be offended by it. I had learned it was futile to challenge such expressions under those circumstances, as futile as objecting to blasphemy or sexual humor, which was also reserved exclusively for male conversation.

But, in this case, once we were out of the seminary students hearing, I angrily challenged Dick for having embarrassed me with such behavior. He began to defend himself with a combination of anthropological and religious distortions of truth, a litany of racial propaganda that I had heard before, but had always considered too laughable or from too unworthy a source to dignify with a response. Now, for the first time, I had to deal with it from someone I had considered an equal, a sixteen-year-old who had reasonable looks, education, apparent manners, and no visible inadequacies which should lead him to compensate at the expense of others. We continued our debate into my house and the presence of Katherine, to whom Dick now appealed to support his argument.

Ultimately I realized I could not sway nor reason with Dick's religious and social training, but what began to concern me more was Katherine's response to the effect that I should allow Dick his particular approach to life and he mine. It was obvious to me that he was not going to allow me my opinion, and it was equally obvious that Katherine shared my opinion, but was not prepared to admit to it or defend it. Through the years she had filled me with all these ideals, yet now she was leaving me all alone to defend them, not willing to risk her own safe neutrality even if I bled alone on the battlefield.

That day I gladly gave up Dick's friendship, but, with far greater regret, I accepted the final evidence that my beautiful, talented, brilliant mother did in fact have certain reservations and limitations. I gave her the benefit of the doubt that she would probably not have defended A.J. in a similar situation.

Perhaps it was the feeling that in life I would have to fight all my battles alone that led me to be such a loner throughout high school. My peers were the usual assortment of good and bad, with a greater ethnic and economic diversity than found in most communities, and a greater measure of tolerance and hardiness which that diversity instilled. Yet I never maintained their friendship after graduation, and mostly what I learned from my school peers was what mistakes should be avoided.

Popularity, romantic attachments, blindly accepting a family tradition of ignorance or prejudice; none of these were worth the importance and sacrifice most of my peers accorded them. I did not share their values nor participate in their rites of passage, and, accordingly, they excluded me from the joys and sorrows of adolescence so completely that in my senior yearbook, despite the many photos I contributed to it and the fact that I did indeed graduate, neither my name nor picture appear.

(Top left) Martin Noto.

(Center right) Odelle Saucier.

(Center left) Thelma Morris in her Patton Street apartment with Buddy.

(Bottom right) Thelma Morris in her jeep in Hamburg.

(Lower left and right) A.J. in his upstairs Patton Street apartment. The copper trays on the wall and bookshelves are his own artwork. The copper and brass dragon shield on top bookshelf he made for his elaborate and authentically recreated Mardi Gras Viking costume. The rapier he holds in his hands is his grandfather's dress sword which Will Schmidt wore at formal Masonic events. The books are a treasury of information on ancient art, Anglo-Saxon history, and the occult, some of which he re-bound in illuminated copper covers.

Chapter Eleven
HURRICANE

Hurricane is a West Indian word for storms originating at sea and developing winds in excess of 75 miles an hour. The term is used in the environs of the Atlantic Ocean, as opposed to the Chinese term Typhoon referring to similar storms in the Pacific. The shallowness of the 1100 by 800 mile Gulf of Mexico not only generates 100 billion gallons of warm water an hour to warm the Atlantic seaboard of North America, Iceland, England, and the north coast of France with the Gulf Stream, it also generates more hurricanes than any other similar body of water in the world.

Hurricanes usually occur in greatest number along the Gulf Coast of North America during the end of Summer. The vicinity of Bay St. Louis usually experiences several smaller hurricanes annually and a major hurricane with winds between 100 to 150 miles an hour approximately twenty years apart. These major hurricanes usually devastate the coastline with millions of dollars in property damage and dozens and sometimes hundreds of lives lost.

For every grey cloud in our environment, there is usually the silver lining of a unique and valuable lesson to be learned. The seemingly deprived inner city child has the rare opportunity to learn the psychology of personal image, competition, and the creation and penetration of personal facades. His country cousin may lack the experience of that social laboratory, but has a far more wholesome opportunity to understand nature, procreation, and a sense of ecological balance. The Coastal child may suffer the uncertainty of living in the path of one of natures most destructive forces, but hurricanes teach that child how tenuous material things are. He sees the rich man's mansion leveled to its footings in a matter of minutes, his yacht thrown miles inland and scattered through the forest like a million toothpicks, and his life as fragile and extinguishable as the poor man's in the face of nature's wrath.

That child learns that life is one third what you know, one third what you do with what you know, and one third luck. Not the kind of luck that lets you win a million dollars in the lottery, but rather the kind of luck that lets you and yours survive the hurricanes in life.

Perhaps there is a correlation between the cycles of nature's hurricanes and those figurative hurricanes in our personal lives. Every year we have our minor hurricanes, and approximately every twenty years we have our major ones. We even approximate the ages of our life in twenty year cycles; childhood the first twenty years, young adult the next twenty, middle age the next twenty, and old age the remaining cycle.

These hurricanes, both the literal ones of nature and the metaphoric ones in our personal lives, also perform another beneficial service. Without the time and trauma of war or pestilence, in one mighty though painful sweep, it wipes the slate clean for a new design, a new direction. Where tradition, in the form of a building or in the person of a prior generation, stood in the way of progress, the hurricane offers the freedom of new choices, new opportunities.

But we are rarely ever prepared for hurricanes, because we can never anticipate them unless we study their long term cycles. Usually a hurricane is preceded by a long and unusual period of calm.

The calm began with the end of World War II. The anxieties of war were lifted for the whole population. Francis Wilson was honorably discharged from the Army Air Corps at Keesler Field and came home to face an idyllic family life he had never known before, and now hoped to share with Katherine. Even I looked forward to a brighter existence without the torment of my hyperactive sister who had moved to Canada to live with her father.

Francis was an auto mechanic and the war years had diminished the auto population as no passenger vehicles had been manufactured for the civilian market for over four years. No one was hiring auto mechanics to repair non-existent automobiles. But Francis had co-owned a repair shop in Detroit before the war and felt he could establish his own shop in the Bay. He used his little bit of mustering out pay to start construction of a 20'x30' building on the rear of our corner lot.

Although we lived in the high elevation central part of town, the rear of our lot was a low spot for the immediate neighborhood. There had once been an open drainage stream that ran across the rear of the lot, but by 1945 had been enclosed with poorly engineered and poorly constructed underground wooden culverts fed by uncovered storm drains. The seasonal rains along the coast were often torrential and the drains were more often clogged and ineffectual. At these times our backyard looked like a small lake and as small children we could actually go boating in the tin washtub amid floating clumps of plant debris where bullfrogs sang a guttural serenade.

Francis had never seen our backyard during the rainy season, and he stubbornly ignored Katherine's warnings about the water level to be anticipated. He had only enough money to build the concrete foundation for his shop, and the very first job he attempted on it occurred at the very beginning of the rainy season. He had completely dismantled the vehicle's engine and drive train across the entire exposed concrete floor, only to see one afternoon's rain submerge it all in two feet of water. He eventually got the vehicle back together and running, but it took him many times longer to correct the damage done by water.

There was a noticeable Italian population in the Bay, but Francis was not a blood relative of local families and, although he was warmly accepted by Katherine's friends, he felt estranged by the community that more readily accepted their husbands and sons returning from service than the newcomer, particularly when it came to jobs.

I did not help Francis' sense of alienation. Although A.J. and I had intellectually accepted the positive element that Francis represented in Katherine's life, A.J. was eight years more mature and lived and worked in New Orleans. I, on the other hand, was a twelve-year-old who discovered my mother's marriage meant dividing her attentions and affections and losing all contact with her when her bedroom door closed at night.

Francis made an excellent effort to be a father to me. He attempted to teach me what he knew and I learned to grind auto engine valves by hand, spinning the valve in the block by means of a rubber suction cup on a stick much like the suction cup darts we'd shoot in spring loaded toy guns. He shared his photographic magazines with me and told Katherine that, when things were better, he'd buy me a Kodak 35mm camera like he had once owned in Detroit. He tried to include me in his passion for fishing, but I had long ago been discouraged by the poor success we had with poor man's fishing tackle and borrowed crab nets, and I enjoyed the pictures in *Field And Stream* more than the glamour of fly rods and spinning lures.

For a soft-spoken gentle man, Francis had a sense of 'manliness' that my twelve-year-old body, still slightly swollen with baby fat, did not live up to. His attempts to 'toughen me up' sometimes tested my acceptance of him. In the summer he devised an outing with a couple who lived in the country and whose thirteen-year-old daughter and eleven-year-old son had few nearby playmates. We drove miles across the dry red clay roads to their isolated cottage before it was announced that we children would go fishing for a few hours before dinner.

We set out on foot at midday to the fishing stream which was 'a few miles' away. The red headed freckle faced girl was eager to please me, but as mile after mile dragged on across the sun scorched red clay fields, I found it increasingly difficult to hide my exhaustion and irritation. When we reached the stream, I could do nothing more than lay in its shallow waters until the other two children admitted defeat in catching anything, and we started back.

The girl was apologetic and ultimately confessed that Francis had suggested days before that I be led on this ten mile round trip hike as part of a fitness program he had in mind for me. I arrived back at the house exhausted and filled with silent anger which precluded any friendship with the children or positive participation by me for the rest of the day.

Francis was amazed by the contrast of how much I knew about biology and the clinical realities of procreation, and how little I knew about sex. I remember coming back from swimming and complaining to my mother about the awkward habit my body had of producing erections when I was swimming with my female peers, honestly not understanding the sexuality involved. Francis looked at Katherine and rolled his eyes, unable to believe my innocence.

He also found it difficult to understand the expressions of affection I shared with Katherine. Katherine had a penchant for sensual fabrics; silks, satins, tulles, and velvets. My desire to be close to and hugged by her was equal to my desire to wallow in the exciting fabrics and fragrances which comprised her wardrobe and bedroom furnishings. He found it questionable that I be allowed to put on her jewelry and silk bathrobe and swish the fabric around me obviously delighting in its feel on my bare skin. I'm sure Katherine indulged me in this behavior in a conscious effort to compensate me for the division of her affections.

Katherine managed to maintain a truce between us, but Francis was obviously suffering through a transitional period both into civilian life and family life. He did amazingly well for a man, barely forty, who had never had to deal with children or the economic depression of the time and locale in which he found himself.

But, ultimately, his decision was to re-enter the service where he had a guaranteed income and a degree of isolation from the household. He lived at Keesler field and came to the Bay on weekends, which lessened the tensions for all. Within a year of their marriage, Francis was stationed in Alaska where he had an aunt, the only known relative since his childhood days in the orphanage. We never knew if he had requested the transfer or not. He sent Katherine jewelry made of walrus tusk ivory and gold nuggets, and snapshots of him with his aged aunt.

Francis had only been in Alaska a few months when Katherine got notice he was in an army hospital in Houston, Texas. When she arrived there he was in a coma. He had been hospitalized as a mental patient. He had simply taken to walking off duty and going fishing. He never gave anyone any trouble, he simply explained that he wanted to go fishing. Shortly after he had been hospitalized for observation, he slipped into a coma.

Little more than a year after their marriage, Francis Blaine Wilson died without ever coming out of the coma. He was buried in the Bay St. Louis public cemetery, the same one great grandmother Mimi was buried in, with a bronze headstone provided by the military and a ragged row of VFW performing a taps ceremony replete with rifle shots.

Katherine derived many benefits from the marriage, perhaps the greatest being the reaffirmation of her self image as a woman. Even though Francis was several years younger than her, he had found her desirable enough to commit himself to marriage. He had introduced her to the physical joys of mutual love and sexual satisfaction she had not known before. He had been a partner, sharing the burdens of survival and parenting, even if the attempt had not always been completely successful. And there were the more literal benefits; the erasure of old debts, the long needed repairs to the house, and the long needed surgery she received shortly after their marriage and she enjoyed the benefits of a military dependent.

That was a time when the medical profession did not bother to explain the consequences of a procedure such as a hysterectomy to the patient. It was before the widespread knowledge and practice of hormonal therapy after a hysterectomy. Katherine had always been proud of her svelte dancer's figure, but, within a year after her surgery, she had acquired what looked like an inner tube around her midriff which would stay with her, despite her continual efforts to lose it, the rest of her life.

Another tragedy we experienced during the one year duration of her second marriage occurred when we saw Dr. Horton's old Model T Ford coupe pull up to our fence and were surprised to see a strange young man in overalls exit it and approach Katherine with his hat in his hand. He apologetically explained that Dr. Horton died after being kicked in the head by a mule he was attending. Actually, the good doctor was making a house call on the sick wife of a farmer who, as an afterthought, asked him to look at his ailing mule. Katherine exploded into tears and had to be helped into the house, suffering a depression that lasted for weeks.

I remembered the last time he had treated me for

a bone fellon on my right index finger. The first joint was swollen as big as a robin's egg, and I might well have lost the end of or the entire finger. After suffering for three days with it, Katherine took me to Dr. Horton's house on the beach at night. He frowned at the finger briefly, then told us to go straight to the 'hospital' on Carrol Avenue, the converted residence where Pansy Benoit had died. He joined us there and asked me if I wanted an anesthetic or not before he opened the end joint and scraped the pus laden bone. I hesitated, remembering the painful headaches after the tonsillectomy on Staten Island. Dr. Horton took my silence for a 'no' and picked up a scalpel to make the incision, instructing Katherine to hold me down. I suddenly found my voice and requested the anesthetic. Dr. Horton 'harumphed' and dug out the gauze mask and bottle of ether which he poured a drop at a time while Katherine held my hand reassuringly.

Forever after, the old grey building on Main Street, or the appearance of a Model T Ford coupe, or the scar I carry on the end of my right index finger, inspires warm memories of that cantankerous old man with bushy white hair and liver spots on his face and arms who saved our lives and worked his country doctor miracles for countless people who remember him lovingly.

About this time, Aunt Thelma's life was not faring much better than Katherine's. Aunt Thelma's business success had suffered the liability of Bob Morris' drinking, crass manners, and tactlessness. Her upward mobility in the executive crowd reached a plateau and began to decline as Bob's drunken excesses excluded them from the sophisticated cocktail circuit. She lost the Staten Island house, she was pushing fifty, and she was long overdue for promotions that were not going to come to a female executive with the albatross of a drunken husband around her neck.

Lola's diabetic condition worsened and became

enough of an excuse for Aunt Thelma to give up her job in New York and return to New Orleans to care for her mother. Bob came with her out of habit, even though he had gone through most of her money and she refused to give up what little was left. She worked as a clerk in the New Orleans branch of the exchange for which she had once managed the New York home office.

Bob ran horse wires between long drinking bouts when he would disappear for ever increasing periods of days or weeks or months. This was the period I worked in the New Orleans photo processing plants during my summer vacation and stayed with Lo. I'd sit at the dinner table and watch the silent trio of Lo, Aunt Thelma, and Bob Morris who would try to needle the two women into speaking with stinging asides or off color jokes. He sought to find an ally in me through 'man to man' bonding, but all I could remember of him were his unwelcome advances to Katherine in the basement of the Staten Island house, and I gave him the silent treatment too.

Finally, Bob disappeared for over a year. Aunt Thelma began a seven year vigil before she could legally declare him dead and feel free to once again have assets in her own name. In one sense, everyone felt a great sigh of relief when he disappeared. On another level, though, it was the final admission that a traditional or happy marriage such as Lola had was not going to be in the lives of her two daughters.

Diabetes had taken its toll of Lola, now in her middle sixties and so troubled by her feet she could not climb the stairs to the upstairs apartments. Fortunately, insulin had been discovered, but Lo hated to give herself injections and Aunt Thelma fulfilled that daily chore for her.

Lo had discovered the Rosicrucian religion at this point. She had a pier table in her bedroom that served as an alter with two candlestick holders, black balls on black triangular bases. She would use different colored candles for the various rites she would perform, all based on some mystical formula I suspect was a hybrid of Rosicrucian training and Mimi's lessons in witchcraft.

I was the youngest, the last child to remain at home. Lo was the oldest, having seen her two children survive to midlife with a level of maturity and independence which, while not what she had hoped for them, was none-the-less as wise and as strong as any support she could offer them. Lo developed a passion to make peace with whatever mistakes she had made in life, and to pass on to me whatever wisdom she had sifted from those experiences.

She enrolled me in a children's Rosicrucian mail-order course which couched its spiritual and moral lessons in the traditions and trappings of the American Indian, but I considered it simplistic and plodding compared to the 'secret' adult Rosicrucian materials I had surreptitiously read without anyone knowing.

When I had resisted the efforts of well meaning adults like Uncle Grady or Father Carre or the high-ranking nun at St. Agnes to bend me to what they thought best for me, I had alarmed Lo and Katherine with my despair at the hypocrisy of society. I frightened them by asking questions about the morality of the young mother with melancholia who had blown her brains out, and how painful it might be to commit suicide by poisoning.

In reasoning with me, Lo and her Rosicrucian materials introduced me to two words which encouraged me by proving that others had strayed from conformity and survived. One word was 'eclectic,' from the Greek verb 'to choose,'` and defined as "selecting what appears to be best in various doctrines, methods, or styles." I now knew that the seed of truth I found in different religions and philosophies did not oblige me to submit wholly to their dogma. I could accept and utilize those parts which appealed to my logic without being frustrated by the inconsistencies and incongruities of the whole.

The other word was 'agnostic,' from the Greek noun 'unknowable,' defined as "one who holds the view that any ultimate reality (such as God) is unknown and probably unknowable." This gave me the option to consider the possibility of a spiritual realm without having to commit myself to either religion or atheism.

Now Lo showered more affection on me than she had ever dared to do when my brother and sister lived with us. She took me with her on all her pilgrimages to visit aged friends and the grave sites of the departed. And she sat patiently waiting for me to show the interest or fate to provide the opportunity for her to impart to me the lessons she had learned. To endure the constant changes in life, to be tolerant of faults in ourselves as well as others, and to recognize and appreciate the best of life in its own time and place.

To her daughters she kept saying that she didn't want to be a burden, that fate had been kind to her mother Mimi by taking her peacefully in her sleep with a smile on her face, and she would hope for as much for herself.

Aunt Thelma was in the process of trying to reclaim the remains of the Natchez homestead from the land grabbers and tax sales, hoping to retire to and farm it, and hoping her mother would live to see this accomplished. Katherine's children were not married or successful, and she hoped her mother would live to see those achievements.

Less than a year after Francis Wilson's death, Lo died of a cerebral hemorrhage, not in her sleep as she had hoped, but without prolonged pain and within the span of a few days illness. Her funeral in New Orleans was attended by an impressive number and diversity of people, and she was buried beside her husband, Will Schmidt, in the cemetery we had visited so often in the years just before her death.

In less than two years Katherine lost her daughter to Earl in Canada, her firstborn son left home seeking work, Dr. Horton was the victim of an unappreciative mule, her second husband slipped into a terminal coma, and her mother died. I was the only one left to her, and my efforts to fill that void in her life were sorely inadequate.

I was thirteen. The baby fat had all melted away as I grew to my full 5'11" height, and I looked ten-years-older than my true age. For several years my efforts to impress Katherine with my music, photography, and income producing enterprise had met with muted praise until finally she suggested to me that I should not "blow your horn too loud as there are others who cannot equal your accomplishments through no fault of their own." I realized she was referring to my brother who, until he left home, was a recluse hiding away in his pipe smoke filled room amid his medical drawings and specimens, reading voraciously, but never interacting with the outside world.

I recognized that the zeal Katherine had poured into the survival of her firstborn child and, perhaps, the guilt she felt at having exposed him for nine years to the psychological harm done by his father, created a bond between Katherine and A.J. that I would never know with my mother. I also recognized I would never know the bond she had found with Francis which had blossomed in one short year and which excluded me from her time and her touch. Now that we were alone together, it was not as mother and son, but rather as two acquaintances in limbo; she facing the diminishing options of her future, and I without access to my growing options as an adult.

I threw myself into my photography, having just bought my first press camera and identifying with the comic strip character 'Flashgun Casey' who was a photojournalist observing the violence of the world without having to judge or participate in it. I realized that rewards and recognition would have to come from the external world rather than my family. My family was extremely adept at preparing me for life, but ill prepared to support me either materially or psychologically. I remembered one of Lo's favorite poems she had read to me one sunny afternoon on the front porch of Patton Street when I had complained of my aloneness in life's struggles. It read:

> TO BLEED ALONE
> *anonymous*
> *Our crosses are hewn from different trees*
> *but we all must have our calvaries*
> *Though we climb the height from a different side*
> *but we each go up to be crucified*
> *As we scale the steps another may share*
> *the dreadful load our shoulders bear*
> *But the costliest sorrow is all our own*
> *for on the summit we bleed alone.*

But behind a piano or a camera I was the darling of the external world. I was the fulfillment of their fantasies constructed in the simplistic lyrics of pop songs or the glamorous photographic renditions of their physical beauty or prowess. Now the high school sex queens tried to charm me into photographing them in all their cheerleader and drum majorette glory, and the high school jocks buddied with me more than I really desired in hopes I'd photograph their athletic adventures for the school paper or yearbook. At first I wallowed in the acceptance, but quickly saw through the veneer to the reality that most of society was structured according to who had money, clothes, and cars, and I neither had nor respected the behavior of most who had such assets.

I longed for the opportunity to apply my talents to

something more profound. I considered entering the clergy, but rejected all the religiosity I had been exposed to as hypocritical. I enjoyed music, but found my interests too diverse to make the all consuming commitment of a classical pianist, and I regarded pop music as infantile. Photojournalism seemed the logical course, but photographing cheerleaders and high school athletics was as superficial as pop music in my eyes.

I sometimes digest my axiom that life is one third what you know, one third what you do with what you know, and one third luck, to simply talent, perseverance, and luck. It is hard for adolescents to persevere when hormones and horrifying pictures of atomic mushroom clouds are telling them there may not be a tomorrow, that their mission in life is to insure the survival of the species here and now. Perhaps I was fortunate that, for whatever reason, my hormones did not kick in too early and distract me from preparing for life with my various talents, including the talents to observe and learn. I persevered until luck, in all its devious and sometimes malevolent form, appeared on the scene.

On September 19, 1947, before the days of assigning names to them, a hurricane of gigantic proportions headed for the Gulf Coast with winds up to 150 miles an hour, and its path tracked directly for the Bay of St. Louis. This was a time when meteorologists could not predict the intensity nor imminence of a storm with any degree of accuracy or forewarning. By early morning, however, we knew we were in for a big one as the edge of the hurricane arrived and began peeling the tin and slate roofs off the houses on our block with enough ferocity to cleave slate shingles from a block away completely through our 1 ½"x14" wooden step treads. Katherine and I huddled in the center hall of the cottage to avoid the flying glass as tree limbs, bricks, and other debris flew through the windows.

On the pretext of going to the bathroom, I peered

through the bathroom window at the three young trees, each 12" or more in diameter, which bordered the fence between the two cottages. Every leaf had been stripped from them as they flayed back and forth in a frenzied ballet, their branches touching the ground as if kowtowing to the winds of the North, South, East, and West. A small twister traveled a wavering path from the backyard, vacuuming up small plants and tin cans and bottles filled with rainwater as if they were leaves. As it hit the wire fence, it began to travel in a straight line and, one by one, twisted each of the three trees into a corkscrew, their twisted trunks growing like that forever after.

The adrenalin in my veins screamed at me to do something. I guess I felt like a soldier in a foxhole pinned down by an enemy machine gun until fear and frustration pump him up enough to break out of the foxhole and storm the machine gun nest. But, trapped in the shaking shuddering cottage, my enemy had no shape or location that I could attack.

Suddenly I sensed that a great event was taking place, and, as a photographer, I was the most qualified person to record it. My place was out THERE, in the thick of the storm, camera in hand. I gathered my gear as Katherine watched me in amazement. As I put on my raincoat, it dawned on her what I intended to do and she pulled at my sleeve as I opened the front door, the wind and water pushing her back with such force she tore my sleeve. Hugging my folded camera beneath my coat, I implored her, "Please, mother. I must go to the beach."

She looked at me wide-eyed, rainwater dripping from her face. "You'll be killed!"

I heaved a big sigh and said, "No, mother, I wont be killed. I'll be very very careful."

She shook her head from side to side. "You'll be killed, and I have already lost so much. Don't do this to me."

I heaved another sigh and said, "Mother, I'm not doing this to you. I'm doing this for me."

She looked at the torn piece of coat sleeve in her hand, and then back up at me with what might pass as a pained smile, saying, "Of course, I'm sorry. You want to take your pictures."

She turned to re-enter the hall, then turned back to me and said, "Please, son. Please be careful."

I smiled and answered, "Of course. Don't worry, I wont be long." Then I turned and shut the door.

The screen door was already gone, the screens ripped from the porch together with the porch furniture which could not be found in the front yard. The wisteria arbor was stripped of every single blossom and swayed back and forth like a labyrinth of snakes dancing the Tarantella. I turned down Second Street toward Main Street, but had gone only a few feet when I saw a sheet of roofing tin flying about fourteen feet off the ground with an undulation rather like the large manta rays we'd sometimes see gliding underwater as we swam in the Bay. The sheet of tin, however, was traveling faster than any manta ray I'd ever seen and came to rest only after it had cleaved a telephone pole in half like slicing through butter.

Suddenly I felt scared, thinking of what the sheet of tin might have done to me. I looked at my house and saw Katherine's face appear in the front window. I wondered if she saw the sheet of tin knife through the telephone pole. I smiled wanly at her and pushed on toward Main Street.

As I approached the two cross streets that led to the beach, tremendous gusts of air roared toward me like wind tunnels. I could see the crests of waves at the beach end of the block, even though the land at that point was thirty feet above sea level. I considered going down them, but they did not offer the picture potentials Main Street and the intersection of Main and Beach Boulevard afforded.

Down DeMontluzin Boulevard, the first cross street, I saw 300-year-old mammoth oak trees strain and bend and keel over, the immense circle of their root structures rising out of the ground half as high as the erect trees had been. I wondered with concern if Tarzan Oaks or the large Oak tree beside our house would survive.

Down State Street, the next cross street, I saw an empty 1939 Ford coupe traveling sideways, its tires folded up under the fenders and its rims gouging troughs in the blacktop. In the front yard of the house the Squaw Man had once lived in, I saw the remains of the wicker chaise lounge from our front porch floating in a large pool of rainwater together with chairs and doors and a large rubber doll that smiled up at the churning sky.

Traversing the intersection of the cross streets, I had to lean at a 45 degree angle into the wind coming from the beach. When I reached Main Street, the long block to the beach had to be negotiated leaning at a 45 degree angle into the wind and tacking back and forth with each fluctuation of the wind. There was less residential property in that last block of Main Street before the beach, so there was less flying furniture, doors, roofing slates and tin to dodge. The wood frame buildings like the Methodist church, Mrs. Charmichael's building, and Dr. Horton's office had lost a few clapboards, but were more or less intact. The masonry government buildings like the county court house and post office looked relatively unscathed, and I began to think I might not get any newsworthy pictures.

As I reached the head of Main Street and Beach Boulevard, my doubts were allayed. I was facing what appeared to be the vortex of hell. The sea level had risen more than twenty feet and some waves were cresting another twenty feet above that. The sky overhead was black and visibility across the water came and went as the rain came in dense sheets for minutes at a time, then disappeared for minutes as tunnels of air blasted toward me with clear vision of the boiling waters, the distant lightening, and the havoc to the toy like structures of man.

The south end of the beach business district was bordered by the L&N railroad tracks, the tracks continuing on a wooden bridge that spanned the two miles across the mouth of the bay to Henderson Point. The bridge swayed sideways like a water moccasin dancing across the waters. When vision permitted, you could see that about every twentieth wave was a mini-tidal wave, and these caused the bridge, already almost under water, to undulate up and down as well as its continuous sideways gyrations. As the heart of the hurricane moved closer, the mini-tidal waves came more frequently; every twelfth wave, then tenth and eighth and sixth.

The buildings on the landward side of Beach Boulevard were mostly substantial masonry buildings of more recent construction such as the two bank buildings and the A&G Theater. The buildings on the beach side of the road, however, were all very old single story wood frame buildings built on pilings over the sloping cliff that dropped thirty or more feet down to the normal waterline.

The northernmost beach side structure in the two blocks of the business district was Hamburger Heaven where I used to fetch quart bottles of coffee for Mr. Zerr in the projection booth of the A&G theater across the street. There were several bars, some offering keno and other games of chance where squealing housewives lost their household money on regular nights of the week, contrary to the supposed laws of the land. In some of these bars, A.J. had whetted his appetite for alcohol and befriended World War II servicemen.

There were the two fish stores, the Bay Fish Store

and the Red Star Seafood Market, both with piers leading directly out the back of the store to boat sheds several hundred feet into the water where dozens of rowboats and an occasional shrimp boat were usually moored. In their smelly showrooms speckled trout, red snapper, sheep head, flounder, catfish, and deep sea bass looked up with hypnotic round eyes from their icy beds, and live crabs played a continual game of King of the Mountain in their deep tin lined counter.

There were three drugstores, the oldest of which was deMontluzin's founded in 1878 by the son of one of Napoleon's elite officers and then operated by the grandson and great grandson, Rene Sr. and Rene Jr., the latter a member of Katherine's string quartet. The structure was rebuilt in 1897 after a fire, its curved glass and marble counters displaying tempting assortments of penny candies and gift boxes. Just inside each of the two front doors were larger than life-size turn of the century posters, one of a lady fancily dressed from her befeathered broad rimmed hat to her high button shoes as she enjoyed a Coca Cola, another of a lady as fully covered by her underwear while she applied a Blue Bird Corn Plaster to a shockingly uncovered foot.

Through the turned wood lattice at the rear of the store, one could see shelf upon shelf of large glass bottles with large ground glass stoppers containing exotic raw ingredients which would be ground by hand with mortar and pestle to compound Dr. Horton's vintage remedies. If one were lucky, one might see Rene Sr. open such a bottle to remove live leeches which he expertly applied to the puffy blue lower eyelids of a patient reclining on a chaise lounge in the apothecary, usually one of the older barkeeps.

DeMontluzin's drugstore was the second building from the L&N tracks on the beach side, and, as I turned the corner from Main Street onto Beach Boulevard, my first view of the horizon was through the glass showcase of the drugstore as the rear half of the building housing the apothecary had been torn away to reveal a view of the railroad bridge and the Gulf beyond.

I was hypnotized briefly by the dancing bridge, its rails, normally twenty feet above the water, now rising and falling beneath the water like an impression of the Loch Ness monster. A large section of the bridge broke away and began to travel across the waves toward the town. The section must have been about forty feet, the rails at either end dangling like lamp cord as it bobbed up and down in the water until it arrived on shore and began to chew away the backs of the old wood frame buildings like a wrecking ball.

I cautiously unfolded my camera, keeping my back to the wind and the camera under my coat until I saw a clear shot. I had a haze filter over the lens which had to be wiped clean before each exposure, plus changing the film holders with great difficulty and having to chase after a dark slide when the wind ripped it out of my hand. I learned to time the mini-tidal waves and wait for the peak moment when the bridge section would rise into the air like a prehistoric monster and cleave into a building, or when a floating telephone pole or large boat would take smaller slices as it was tossed on the crest of a wave and landed on the roof of one of the sagging structures. Sometimes a building would just slip away like a boat being launched or a sand castle being pulled out by the tide. That's when my shutter would click.

I was knocked down repeatedly by wind and debris, but luckily suffered only minor bruises. The eye of the storm arrived with the false impression of sunlight and calm, the bay turning almost glassy smooth despite its strange high water level, reminiscent of Drysdale's scenic paintings of calm lakes highlighted by narrow shafts of sunlit slicing through the dark skies. Then the tail of the hurricane arrived and unleashed hell again.

I regretted that I only owned seven film holders and, as the tail of the hurricane began to wane and I exposed my last sheet of film, I folded my camera beneath my coat and began a cautious return to the cottage. Of the fourteen shots I made that day, almost every one was worthy of *Life Magazine,* although I was too naive to think that big. I was thinking more in terms of local and New Orleans newspapers which had bought my shots of the burning Audubon Park stables. Two days later I had processed the negatives, but we had no electricity to make prints as most of the coast was devastated and under martial law, and I had no way to market my pictures.

In our county alone the hurricane had destroyed hundreds of buildings, damaged over a thousand more, injured hundreds of people, and taken twelve lives. I realized I had taken a great risk, and I felt fortunate to still be alive.

On the second day after the hurricane and before I had a chance to print my processed negatives, a little man with a narrow face and a baggy seersucker pinstripe suit came to our house and said he had heard I took pictures during the storm. After looking at my processed negatives, he offered me $100 for the lot of them, twice what *The Times Picayune* had paid me for the burning stable shots, and, as a fourteen-year-old novice, I took it.

He also offered me a job working in his darkroom where he made postcards of the disaster. He came from 'Tornado Alley' in Oklahoma with his trailer full of photo equipment and his thin little wife, and he had made a lifetime career of following disasters, manufacturing postcards of the event, and selling them both wholesale and retail.

I assisted him as he visited the worst sites of destruction, photographed them on his 5"x7" Graflex camera, and returned to process them in the damaged but serviceable frame building he had rented across from the court house. I learned how to copy prints of my own photos on his 5"x7" view camera in order to have a postcard sized negative, print the captions on the negatives with a handset rubber stamp, and contact print the final postcards on a handmade wooden printer of his own unique design. The postcards were then dried on wooden racks of stretched cheesecloth which he would build and abandon at whatever site in which he was working. After most of the postcards were manufactured, he paid me to sell them retail on the highway, just as I had sold Mrs. Kenny's pralines, while he wholesaled them to drugstores and tourist shops along the coast.

The little man in baggy clothes taught me more than just another stage in the technology of photography. He also taught me how naive I had been to accept the first offer for my pictures, as I saw him sell and resell publication rights to my photographs for many many times what he had paid for them. But I did not regret having sold the pictures nor the risks I took in making them. Instead I valued the experience of his tutelage, the contribution I had made to archiving that event, and the adventure of taking a risk for the sake of art and history rather than foolhardiness.

The 1947 hurricane did not wipe the slate clean for all people. DeMontluzin rebuilt an identical structure on the very same site, as did many others. Some people continued in the same locations with the same traditions; right or wrong, good or bad, wise or not.

Katherine's life changed, however. She had lost everyone else before the hurricane, and with it she sensed that she had lost me. We no longer pretended that she regarded all her children as she did her firstborn. From that point forward she did not feel obliged to hide her total preoccupation with salvaging A.J. from alcoholism. With her bulging abdomen and the newfound independence of her youngest child, she had prematurely entered old age.

And, while I had not made a fortune with my hurricane pictures, I had made a peace with the fear of the future. I had faced death and, with equal trepidation, I had faced my mother, and I had survived. The 1947 hurricane had, for me, created a new beginning. From that point forward, if not a man in every sense, I was, at the very least, my own man.

(Above) The day after the 1947 hurricane. Two-story building in center is where author stood. Domed building at upper right is Court House. Two-story building second from right, is the A&G Theater. Gaps between beachfront buildings are where buildings were totally demolished or slipped out to sea like a boat. *(Upper left)* Remains of DeMoultlizen's Drugstore with railroad bridge at right and fishing piers at left. *(Below)* Beachfront buildings. Fifty-eight years later, Hurricane Katrina would remove the entire business district, most of Beach Boulevard, and re-contour the shoreline.

In the span of one year, Katherine would lose her husband, Francis Wilson *(at left)* and her mother, Lola, shown below, sharing her last Christmas with her daughters Katherine and Thelma, seen with her collie, Buddy. The tree in the Bay cottage was assembled on the living room wall from cedar branches and decorated with Katherine's handmade ornaments and Lola's ivory manger figures in center.

Chapter Twelve
MY TEACHERS

Wisdom is the art of recognizing everyone and everything around us as our teacher. Those we give the various formal titles of 'teacher' to are usually qualified in one small area of life and are empowered, not by the institutions that presume to qualify them, but by each of us based on our need to know and our willingness to learn. A teacher is only as good as their student's desire to learn, and most teachers are primarily inspired by that student's desire.

My ability to learn was not phenomenal in any academic sense. Despite the testing that caused me to be bumped ahead a few classes, my grades in school were little more than average. Even as a child I recognized many of my school teachers as less skilled at teaching than members of my family. I had been so desensitized to approval and reward that the desire to learn had to come from an internal curiosity and fascination with how things, tangible and intangible, worked. If a teacher was not able or willing to indulge my interest in the broader concept of what they were trying to teach me, then we were not a successful learning team when it came to the detailed rote with which they flogged me.

My family was my first and foremost faculty of teachers. Katherine was far ahead of her time, inspired by her desire to be a parent and spurred even farther by the especial needs of her firstborn, she studied all the psychological, medical, and lay texts of the day on parenting. She made a total commitment to being a full time mother and father, and nothing, not even her own mother, came before her children. Her background talents and family trappings provided the instructional media hardware for a learning process where sight and sound and hands-on training were a part of the daily home environment.

The family library provided not only a ready reference, but the habit of verifying beyond any doubt and a consensus of opinion beyond mere speculation. If an illustration did not exist in the book, our hands did more than gesture, we drew and colored and molded a reality far more convincing than vague descriptions and nebulous ideas. If we could not build a life size castle of wood and stone, then we could build it in miniature with cardboard and papier mache. If we could not fulfill a desire in reality, then we could fantasize with pencil and paint. If we could not literally fly out of a geographical and economical pit, then we could soar on the wings of music and dance and imagination.

One of Katherine's greatest learning tools was games. Formal games, like the bamboo and ivory Mah Jong set that came out of the beautifully carved wood case, were obvious mathematical 'flash cards' with some social symbolism much like a western deck of cards, but much more exotic and glamorous. Scrabble and Monopoly and chess were staples with obvious social significance which most families of that day enjoyed. But Katherine invented games to meet the particular needs of her children.

Her 'Tarzan Lunches' were typical of her innovation. We learned many aspects of zoology and ecology hunting down the animal bedecked brown paper bags with spear and bow and arrow in our hands, even though it began as a desperate attempt to keep us from feeling bored and deprived with our endless diet of baloney sandwiches. Our backyard became the jungles of Africa, the mountains of Tibet, and the frozen frontier of the Arctic.

The worn Persian rug in our living room, where she would let us draw chalk circles and play marbles on a cold winters day, would sometimes become Ali Baba's magic carpet and each child would take a turn sitting on it and telling the tale of where it would fly in their imagination to all the wondrous lands and peoples depicted in the outdated copies of National Geographic we inherited from friends. The story related by one child's experience reading an article in a book or magazine would not only share that particular knowledge with the others, but spur the listeners to research the family library so they were prepared to pilot the magic carpet.

Katherine was challenged to help her children escape the reality that they were poor and hungry, but when the issue could no longer be avoided, Katherine invented a game that predated the television series *The Millionaire,* or the invention of television, by decades. It was probably inspired by those 'chance' cards in the Monopoly game: "Stock Dividend, you collect $100," "Your Uncle died, you inherit $500." I only remember it started one bleak supperless night when we were all bemoaning our poverty, and Katherine said, "Well, you might have a fortune, someday. Let's prepare you to deal with that, because it has its responsibilities, too. Let's pretend that each of you has just inherited a million dollars, and each one in turn will tell exactly how they'll spend it."

Perhaps that "responsibility" part crept in because there was the extreme long shot that Uncle Grady would adopt me or the family would strike oil on the Natchez homestead, but, initially, the game inspired materialistic visions of filling our bellies and filling the gap between our poverty and the affluence of our family friends. Slowly, each child's greed would give way to spending "the rest on charity." By the time the game had been played dozens of times over the years, we had all become philanthropists funding explorations and endowing research in universities.

I think the most valued aspect of Katherine's rapport with children was that she was not condescending. She did not regard children as a category of inferior humans, as in "and here are the children and pets." Perhaps Lo's attitude that "children should be seen and not heard" inspired Katherine to never so dehumanize children herself. She never expected or demanded a child to perform as or assume the responsibility of an adult, but she never denied them the option to do so if they so chose. She addressed them verbally, solicited their input, and deferred to their valid offerings the same as she did to adults, and most of those children appreciated and tried valiantly to live up to that level of human respect. Certainly all of them loved her; the neighborhood children, the many children whose lives she enhanced while working for the WPA and traveling through the rural areas, and the three children to whom she gave birth.

In contrast, Lo's dictatorial approach did not inspire the same intellectual response from children as Katherine's. Having your mouth washed out with Octagon soap with no better explanation of your wrongdoing than "you know why" was almost cruelly frustrating and sometimes even counterproductive. But the Octagon soap, occasional switches, and less occasional threats of even worse did instill a kind of discipline which proved helpful in later years when dealing with similar 'Catch 22' systems like bureaucracies or the military. "He who can keep his head while all about him are losing theirs" may possibly have had a Germanic disciplinarian somewhere in their background.

Lo did teach me a kind of self discipline and a respect for those authorities which prove themselves valid in time, few as they may be. Whether it is accepting the leadership of a gifted director or artist, or conversely risking one's job or very life in defying an unworthy authority, there is a remnant of Lo's 'tough love' that has helped me steel myself to the job at hand many times in life. Of course, in her final years, Lo was the one who showed me the various options of spiritual philosophies available to me, and, by her example, that one can endure loneliness and accepting their own mistakes in life.

Aunt Thelma taught me that a woman can perform in any field a man can, from managing an international office successfully to plowing a field with a four wheel drive jeep. She taught me that economics is a tool of the mind on which no gender or race or ethnic group has any monopoly. She also taught me that romance can turn your brain to silly putty and that you can survive those mistakes of the heart, but sometimes only at such a considerable expense of time and money that it can change the course of your life.

A.J. taught me a great many things, from being a fair chess player to having a vocabulary steeped in esoterica and the occult. From him I learned that men can romanticize more than just physical love; they can romanticize whole cultures as if they had been intentionally designed by wise men rather than just haphazardly evolved, and whole institutions such as war as tools of this design rather than just greedy grasping for power. A.J. was a living lesson that talent and intelligence could not necessarily save you from self delusion, disillusionment, and self destruction.

My sister, Thelma, taught me that strength, endurance, and persistence were to be found in both genders, and that these seeming virtues could be used for better or for worse. Like A.J., she taught me that the fulfillment or frustration of parental attachments were not a valid substitute for the search for one's own identity. She was so much better and so much worse than other women I've known, that she dispelled any misconception that women were a predictable category of humans defined by 'feminine' traits.

Each family friend added to the wealth of learning the especial lessons of their particular talents and travails. The good intentions of Uncle Grady and the vain ambitions of his domineering wife, Sadie. The humanity of Dr. Horton hidden beneath the mask of a crotchety old man. The Jekyll of Bob Bumgarner in symbiotic imbalance with the Hyde of Bob Morris. The good country mother of Mrs. Goldman and the colorful absentee father in the Commodore. The good father and culinary talents of Joe Church and his wife. The femininity of Rosalie and the superstitions of her mother, Mrs. Pienas. The cultural contributions of Adeline Knoblock and the strength and tenacity of Caroline Keifer. The merchants and tenants and individuals too numerous to mention, yet each had some virtue or liability that was a lesson waiting to be learned, and I was fortunate enough to inspire some of them to teach me.

And then there were those who society called 'teachers.' My piano teachers; the eccentric Natalie Pienas, the patient Mrs. Weber, and the stern Mrs. Smith. My elementary teachers, all of whose names I cannot remember. Miss Livinia Sellier taught the second grade, lived across the street, and, despite being a very attractive young woman, never married. I was bumped up to Mrs. Sputoni's third grade for such a short time I remember little of her. Mrs. Anderson was a mature grey haired German lady who taught fourth grade and was strong on mathematics.

Miss Campbell, ah, Miss Campbell initiated the first hormonal throbbings of my puberty in the fifth grade and left me with a subliminal lifelong weakness for fair skinned red headed Irish lasses. For her I published my first hand printed and illustrated weekly class newspaper thumb tacked to the classroom bulletin board regularly in search of her praise and approval. I was disconsolate when she married and moved into the renovated house where the Squaw Man had once lived, the one where our porch furniture and a child's doll floated in the flood of water during the 1947 hurricane.

In the sixth grade, another red headed Irishwoman in the person of Mrs. Dubuisson affected my life by recognizing my academic frustrations and helping me to skip to the eighth grade. Mrs. Georgette Hall taught the eighth grade and, together with Mrs. Dubuisson, would later be among my better high school teachers.

Despite the fact that, in those days, Mississippi and North Dakota had the lowest educational standards in the nation, and despite the fact that the public school I attended was officially and popularly considered to be vastly inferior to the local parochial schools, the structure of high school offered new vistas and new hope to a child graduating from the stagnating format of elementary school. Back then, an elementary teacher was like a general practitioner; one teacher for each grade, one teacher locked in a room with twenty or thirty students for five or six hours a day, one teacher attempting to cover all three bases of 'reading and writing and arithmetic' with very little time or energy left for much more.

How refreshing to enter high school; a place staffed by 'specialists' such as a teacher who only taught English or math or history or science, a place where each day a student came in contact with five or six different teachers and had five or six chances of having a good one for an hour or more, a place where there were such things as 'electives.'

Of course, music had always been one of my electives even before high school, but I had always been a soloist. The high school band directors, however, taught me the art of the ensemble. Pat Rooney, my first band director, taught me to 'vamp,' the trick of reading chord symbols, 'lead sheets,' and 'fake books.' Looking somewhat like a penguin with his slicked back blue black hair, large nose, and slightly rotund body, he would spin the top of my three legged piano stool until it was high enough for his diminutive frame, and spread out the 'charts' of music on my old upright piano. He showed me the musical shorthand that popular dance bands used which my previous classical oriented teachers considered blasphemous, beginning with the cryptic geometric chord symbols used in early hymnals and evolving through the letter chord symbols based on the root triad and modified by diminishing, augmenting, or adding a sixth or seventh or major seventh. This new approach to keyboard harmony made popular music, jazz, and 'playing by ear' available to me and enabled me to form trios and quartets and play the road houses throughout my high school years.

My next band teacher, Mr. Wembly, was also diminutive, but thin and blonde, and he did not actually succeed in getting me to participate in the high school band. He, his wife, and baby, were our tenants in the next door cottage, and, while he did teach me some things musical, he taught me more about photography than music. He had returned from World War II with an Exacta 127 single lens reflex camera acquired when his army unit entered Dresden, Germany, where the Exacta factories had been devastated by allied firebombing and he managed to 'liberate' this beautiful little camera. He generously loaned me the camera which offered a compactness and versatility my press camera did not, and he extended my knowledge of photography where my stepfather and the postcard photographer had left off.

The mainstays of the high school faculty were Mr. and Mrs. Dubuisson. She headed the commercial department and there were very few boys in the typing classes; I was the only one in my particular class. He taught a variety of classes depending upon the faculties needs each semester. I had him for algebra I and II, geometry, driver's education, and mechanics where I developed an early fascination with electronics.

A tall, well proportioned man with thin black hair and a widow's peak in his receding hairline, he was a very handsome man and many of the high school girls had a crush on him. His gold rimmed glasses and soft spoken voice with a hint of Cajun accent in it, combined with his fatherly and compassionate approach to students, gave one the impression of 'Mr. Chips.'

In those days, male students were often punished with whippings, sometimes administered with a belt and sometimes with a wooden paddle. This onerous task was performed by the Superintendent of Schools, a tall potbellied bald man with an atrophied left arm and a greater interest in sports than academia, by the principal, who never seemed to retain that position for more than a year, by the boys coach, who also was a different man every year, and most reluctantly by Mr. Dubuisson.

It would often occur in the principal's office adjacent to Mr. Dubuisson's math class. Sometimes we would hear the tearful appeals of the guilty student, although most of the macho types made a game of refusing to cry out before, during, or after their chastisement. We would hear the resounding smack of the belt or paddle, guessing at who the culprit might be and counting the strokes which varied from five to twenty five. A tribute to Mr. Dubuisson was that students hated to receive their punishment from him most of all. Not that he was any more or less severe in administering it, but because they respected him so much they felt doubly guilty obliging him to do something they knew he abhorred. Perhaps because I had received so many whippings from Lo in earlier years, I managed to avoid such discipline in school.

Mr. Dubuisson both challenged and counseled me more than he did most students. He tried to convince me that mathematics was a medium in which I could express my imagination and interest in abstract concepts, but I did not relate his words to the philosophical and spiritual influence of Lo in time to inspire my math classes. His mechanics class came too late for me to see the relationship of physics and electronics to the cosmos. My interest in electronics ended up mostly being applied to the field of audio recording, and physics merely speculation ultimately expressed by Public Broadcasting Service programs forty years later. But the hint that there was a completely objective language in which both literal and abstract concepts could be expressed, mathematics, was a gift Mr. Dubuisson gave me for which I will forever be grateful.

The teacher that took the most interest in me was Mrs. Curet, a farm wife who had taught in rural schools before moving to town to afford her children a better education, which doesn't say much for the rural schools. In her forties at that time, she had salt and pepper hair, a stocky figure of medium height that had obviously been quite attractive in her youth, and a direct aggressive manner devoid of any sophistication or affectation. She was a good English teacher, but, much more, she was an experienced mother and a sensitive and compassionate human who tuned in to the potentials and problems of each individual student and, as much as the system permitted, attempted to help them.

She helped me even before I entered high school, involving me in the production of the schools first yearbook when I was in the eighth grade, an experience which motivated me to buy my first press camera in order to help make the subsequent yearbooks possible. She put me to work on the school paper, eager to apply the multiplicity of my talents as a photographer, illustrator, and writer. She kept urging me to apply myself in the classes where I displayed little or no interest and made only average grades. The momentum of having someone who believed in and encouraged me might have been more effective if it hadn't been interrupted by my moving to New Orleans in my junior year.

Georgette Hall added to the cultural interests Mrs. Curet had developed in me, although Mrs. Hall's motives were slightly more self serving. She had embarked on a career as a novelist, her first being an ante bellum novel titled *House On Rampart Street* and considered shockingly sexy with numerous scenes of corsets being unlaced and four poster beds shaking and the like. I and a couple of the brightest girls in my class were honored with the tasks of proofreading and retyping an endless succession of new drafts and revisions of the manuscript before it was ultimately published. Although Mrs. Hall did not have Mrs. Curet's experience or intuition, she was a good teacher, and involving us in the creation of her novel was a unique education.

The incident that led Georgette Hall to take most note of me was when she instructed her students to write an essay on anything they wished. I turned in an essay on the mystical ramifications of the number three: the proton, neutron, and electron; the first, second, and third dimensions; male, female, and procreated life; the Holy Trinity; etc.. Thinking, perhaps, that she might enlist more interest and support for a gifted child, she shared the essay with others on the faculty, but metaphysics was not looked on kindly by all in such a small town. While it prompted Mr. Dubuisson to try to interest me in higher mathematics, it led a lot of the faculty to look at me as if I'd grown horns. I became a topic of conversation beyond the school where my spiritual, social, and sexual orientation became suspect.

By my final year of high school, I had grown comfortable in the role of a social maverick. I dressed the part, with a penchant for wearing black, and, at a Halloween costume party, I shocked even the few friends I had by showing up in my usual black, but with my face made up like a woman. I was simply biding my time until I got my high school diploma and was free to leave that small town.

The beginning of the school year in fall of 1949 brought a new teacher into my life, a twenty-three-year-old girl from Alabama who became the librarian at Bay High for one year. The best that I can describe Orrie's appearance is to say she looked like Audrey Hepburn in *Roman Holiday*. Like the naïve princess Audrey played, Orrie was quiet, reserved, and somewhat regal in the way she seemed to glide down the hall rather than jog or bob or weave like most of us. It was an age of long skirts and high necklines, and the first time I saw her she was ascending the stairs before me, her dark taffeta skirt whispering around her well turned ankles and the tightly fitted top of the skirt defining a trim but tantalizing derriere. As she turned at the top landing, she caught me staring at her figure and a guarded smile crossed her face as our eyes met briefly.

Her petite size and youthful appearance made me wonder if she were a new student, but when I entered the library that afternoon, there she was behind the librarian's desk. There was a hesitance before she would respond to anything you said, only a slight movement of her eyebrow or flaring of her nostrils indicating that she had heard you as her mind formulated an answer; sometimes evasive, sometimes sarcastic, always cool and a little officious. Because of her age and size she was challenged to defend herself against the aggressiveness and intimidation of the older boys, but her defensive facade was also born of the fear of attempting her first teaching assignment.

I sensed her vulnerability and wanted to be her protector, and everything about her slim body, shiny black shoulder length hair, and Mona Lisa smile excited a chemistry in me I had never felt before. I asked to use her typewriter for research I was doing, and I thrilled as she hovered around me from time to time, peering over my shoulder at my work and volunteering advice and reference materials.

I knew my body had developed into an impressive figure, my features had matured into an adult image, and my voice had deepened into a manly bass, but I was never fully convinced of the reality or the why of all that coming together until that afternoon I first met Orrie. Before the hour was up, I knew that she was also attracted to me.

I met my intervening class with impatience and reluctance, eager to return to the library before she left. I found her there at the tail end of the last period supervising the shuffling of books around the shelves. I lured her over to one corner of the room on some transparent pretext, the other students curious and confused at the reasonable manner the stern new librarian was exhibiting with me. I wanted to hug her body tightly to mine so bad I was willing to risk being slapped in the face or expelled from school, and the only thing that restrained me was concern for her embarrassment. Instead, I simply asked her, "May I touch you?"

She looked at the distant students staring at us and answered, "I don't think that would be wise."

I countered, "Then, may I hold your hand?"

She looked at the students again, then placed her hand on a bookshelf in front of me out of their sight, saying, "Why is that important to you?"

I looked over my shoulder and glared at the students until they averted their stares, then placed my hand over hers and said, "Because I want to ask you something and, with your hand in mine, I'll know if your answer is true." Then I turned her hand over until our palms met.

She pursed her lips, gave me a condescending smile, and said, "And what is this important question you want to ask me?"

I looked her square in the eye, honestly not knowing what I wanted to ask her until that moment, then I said, "If I asked you to marry me, what would you say?"

Her face dropped into a stunned expression and her hand grew cold in mine. I squeezed her hand gently, feeling the warmth return to it, and she stammered, "I … I can't believe you asked me that."

I pressed her, "But, what would your answer be?"

She took her hand from mine and turned toward the window, leaning against the jam and looking down at the departing students one story below. Finally, she spoke in a slow and measured voice. "No man should ever hear the answer to such a question until that question is asked."

My courage failed me momentarily as I said, "But, if I asked that question, would you reject me because I'm a student or because I'm younger?"

She raised her hand to her mouth, about to bite her fingernail, then realized what she was doing and put both hands firmly on the windowsill, saying, "No woman should reject such a question on those grounds."

I heaved a big sigh, put my hands on her shoulders and turned her around to face me, then said, "Okay, then, will you marry me?"

She turned a frightened face towards the interior of the room and my gaze followed hers, only to learn that we were now alone in the library. The puzzled students had tired of our hushed murmurings and were gone. She put her hands on my upper arms and turned her face to mine, the hint of tears glistening in her eyes. Then she tore herself from me and headed for her desk. I followed her and patiently demanded, "What is your answer?"

She started flinging things from her desk into her purse, saying distractedly, "This is ridiculous."

I placed both hands on her desk and leaned toward her. "Does that mean no?"

She banged her purse down on her desk and looked at me imploringly. "I don't even know you. How can I answer that? How can you ask that?"

I took her right hand in mine and shook it. "Hi! I'm Bill Thomas; precocious problem student. You're Orrie, a beautiful girl and a great librarian. Will you marry me?"

She pulled her hand from mine and smiled resignedly. "Ask me that someday after I get to know you."

I cocked my head and smiled. "Is that a yes?"

She shook her head slowly. "No."

I gave her a mock frown. "Is that a no?"

She thought a moment, then shook her head slowly and smiled, "No."

I walked over and opened the door for her, saying, "Okay, I'll settle for that for the time being. But you better get to know me real fast, because I don't know if I'll survive the whole year."

She looked over her shoulder at me with her Mona Lisa smile as she headed toward the girl's staircase, and I waited until she was out of sight before descending the boy's staircase.

I introduced Orrie to The Little Theater and encouraged her to participate, considering it an ideal cover for the blossoming of our relationship away from the conservative glare of school associates and in the liberal atmosphere of fellow artists. We delighted in the subterfuge like two mischievous children. She dressed in jeans and plaid shirts and most of the theater members thought she was younger and/or I was older, and our horseplay and camaraderie drew no suspicion.

When the production was *The Man Who Came To Dinner,* we had to paint flats with the bookshelves of a library. We giggled as we cryptically titled books such as *For The Love Of Orrie,* by Wilhelm Von Thomas, and *My Secret Passion,* by R. E. Librarian, knowing no one would ever read the painted book spines. Although we restrained any physical or overt expression of our mutual attraction, settling for me helping her up a ladder at the theater or leaning over her shoulder to read something in the library, we shared a growing acknowledgment that a relationship existed between us.

Orrie rented a room from the Greys across the street from the school, the Greys owning a gas station on the opposite corner that had the only hand operated gas pumps in town and the only source of gas during an electrical outage such as a hurricane. The scrutiny of the Greys, who knew me as a Barq's Root Beer and pickled egg customer during school lunch hours, became somewhat uncomfortable as I collected Orrie to work at The Little Theater or assisted her with craft paper and glitter school projects at the Grey's kitchen table.

Finally, Orrie asked me if I wanted to go to the opera in New Orleans with her on the Q.T.. The fact that she was willing to defy the small town propriety was the ultimate admission that we shared a mutually acknowledged relationship. She took the train by herself and I hitchhiked on Highway 90, explaining to my mother that I was visiting friends.

The opera was *Carmen,* which I had seen at the Negro college when the postman had sold Lo tickets, and from which I had played several numbers on the piano, so I was not too provincial in my behavior and responses.

After the concert at New Orleans Municipal Auditorium, we walked through the French Quarter to have coffee and doughnuts at Morning Call in the French Market. Orrie was impressed with my familiarity of the story and score of *Carmen,* and with my knowledge of the history and landmarks of the French Quarter.

As we strolled down Royal Street, admiring the display windows of the worlds greatest concentration of antique stores, we held hands and danced around lamp posts and played hopscotch on the sidewalks paved with ballast stones from ships of old. Neither of us were quite conscious of the fact that we were in love.

In the lobby of the Jung Hotel on Canal Street, I didn't know what to do. I wondered if she would invite me to her room, if I should kiss her in the lobby, or what. Orrie turned to face me as we waited for the elevator. She looked down demurely and said, "Well," as if waiting for me to speak. I took her hands in mine and she looked up and said, "It's been a wonderful evening. Truly, a wonderful evening."

I answered, "Yes, it has," and started to pull her to me. I felt her arms stiffen slightly as she looked down at the deep red carpet again. I let go of her hands, took her right in mine and shook it, saying, "The first of many many more evenings together."

She gripped my hand in both of hers and looked up with a broad smile and somewhat relieved expression, saying, "I'd like that," then disappeared into the elevator.

Teaching in the Bay was the first time Orrie had lived away from home. Although her parents lived in Tuscaloosa, where Orrie attended the University of Alabama, she had lived in a campus dormitory for the convenience and freedom it afforded away from her parents, but they were only a short bus ride away and she visited at home on a weekly basis throughout college.

Her parents had once owned a small farm, but fate or her father's limitations had kept it from being successful, and they eventually moved to the outskirts of the city to eek out their senior years. The oldest son had married and fared well with a job at the local paper mill. The oldest daughter had an atrophied arm which destined her to be an old maid. Orrie was born accidentally late in her parents lives and, perhaps embittered by her husband's lack of success, her mother had not hidden her resentment of the burden of a child born late in life. Still, Orrie loved her father quite strongly and missed her parents and the security of the home she had known in

Tuscaloosa.

The Greys rented a room or two to teachers from time to time, but did not provide board nor a sense of 'family' in their home. At times they were a bit peckish about kitchen privileges, guests, and late hours. I suggested to Orrie that she room and board at my mother's house and, when she appeared delighted at the prospect, I set about convincing Katherine of the idea.

Katherine appreciated the prospect of added income, was flattered Orrie would consider our humble cottage over the somewhat more impressive home of the Greys, and found what she called Orrie's "bird like" personality appealing. I think Katherine was somewhat naive about the potentials of having a young man and woman our ages under the same roof. She moved her things into the middle sized bedroom, invited Orrie to dinner, and the arrangement was sealed.

Katherine soon began to wonder, however, as Orrie and I spent all our time together, teased each other like children, and occasionally ended up rolling around on the living room rug like two puppy dogs discovering the joys of affectionate contact. When Katherine tried to caution us about the propriety of such behavior, we took our horseplay to other locales.

We started to go swimming together down by Tarzan Oaks. There, seeing the wet sheen on her trim and shapely body, feeling her brush against me beneath the water, and feeling the firmness of her flesh as I applied suntan lotion, Orrie and I spoke silent pleas to each other with our eyes as our skin crawled with mutual desire. Touching the fine hairs on her arms and legs, smelling the un-perfumed scent of her wet hair, I became fully conscious of the carnal desires that I had before only understood intellectually.

One day Katherine announced that she had to go to New Orleans regarding apartment house business, saying she would leave Friday morning and return late

Sunday afternoon. She obviously had trepidations about leaving us alone, asking us if she could trust us, and we innocently reassured her.

It rained that Friday. I got home from school first and waited anxiously at the French doors to the living room, my heart quickening as each blurry figure came down the rain swept sidewalk in front of our house. Finally her raincoat clad figure ducked through the overgrown wisteria arbor and into the screen porch. Before she could remove her dripping wraps, I opened the French doors and she stepped inside, pulling the hood from her rain drenched face that stared at me eagerly. I put my arms beneath her coat and crushed her body to mine, her lips to mine, and felt her wet arms encircle me, her body press back against me, and her tongue invade my eager mouth. We both clawed at her raincoat, leaving it in a wet pool just inside the front door. I started to pull her to me again and she pressed me away. I moved back with disappointment in my face and she said, "No. We have to go to my room. Someone will see us through the front door," and with that she opened the door to her room, pulling me in after her by the hand.

In her room we again pressed the length of our bodies together, exploring each others mouths as my hands traveled the length of her back as far as I could reach. We began to press our pelvis's together, like two animals in heat, until I felt bold enough to pick her up and carry her toward the bed. Again she stopped me, saying, "No. I have to change out of these wet clothes." Then, as I set her down in a standing position she added, "You lay down and wait for me."

As she got something from the dresser and retreated to the bathroom, I took off my wet shoes and socks and shirt, and lay down in my pants and undershirt. Soon she returned in panties and a short sheer nightgown and lay down beside me, holding my face between her hands and kissing me tenderly. I got up and removed my pants and undershirt, returning to the bed in my jockey shorts to remove her panties, but, again, she restrained me.

She asked about protection and I produced the two-year-old condom that teen age boys carry in their wallets as a seal of manhood. She took the condom in its cracked tin foil envelope and, with a doubtful look on her face, told me to remove my jockey shorts. She removed the condom from its envelope and attempted to roll it onto my iron hard erection, then the tip of it broke, and I groaned with disappointment. Removing the remnants of the brittle condom, she said, "Don't worry. I can still please you and you can still please me, and there will be other times."

I started to press her to me and she restrained me, saying, "Wait. Do it slowly. Tenderly. Like this." With that she took my hand in hers and moved it slowly over the gossamer covered tips of her small pointed breasts, adding, "We have the whole weekend."

As wind pelted the windowpanes with purple wisteria blossoms and the rain washed them down like a waterfall, a twenty-three year old girl named Orrie showed me how to caress her body and how beautiful it was to have my body caressed by a knowing and caring lover. This was no high school girl feigning ignorance or drunkenness to excuse her own desire. This was not a girl with hypocritical protests that belied the actions and responses of her body. This was a beautiful young woman prepared to honestly declare and share the feelings and desires that filled us both.

We spent the rest of that day and next morning pleasing each other with all the resourceful alternatives to coitus we could devise. It never stopped raining and we never left the house, as much as I wanted to go out in search of condoms.

We lay in each others arms until about noon when we heard the unexpected sound of the front screen door slam. In my awkward confusion, I put my shoes on without lacing them and, clutching my clothes, clambered into the bathroom making an obvious racket. Katherine stepped over Orrie's wet raincoat inside the front door, opened the door to Orrie's room, and saw a guilty looking naked girl clutching a gossamer nightgown to her breast. Katherine shut the door and left the house.

Katherine was resentful, but she was trapped. If she evicted Orrie, it made the whole issue public. If she demanded we desist, it was futile. The best she could do was caution us and monitor us as much as possible. She blamed me bitterly and repeatedly for risking everyone's reputation, and I loudly and hypocritically denied her allegations. It was the only time Katherine and I ever got into real shouting fights, which unfortunately continued throughout most of the last year I was at home.

To complicate matters, A.J. had met Orrie on his infrequent visits to Katherine and, being a more appropriate age for Orrie, had become smitten with her. When Orrie and I asked to stay at the New Orleans apartment when we wanted to go to the opera, Katherine made poor A.J. our chaperon. Orrie and I planned the next visit to the opera as the best opportunity for us to consummate our desire for coitus, but it appeared we wouldn't have any privacy at the apartment.

We decided to skip the opera performance and retreat to Audubon Park in the dark of night. There, in a shrubbery maze with a bronze statue of Diana and her dog looking down at us and a million mosquitoes biting us, I mastered the technology of condoms and technically lost my virginity. I learned, of course, that Orrie had lost hers somewhat earlier in college, but that didn't bother me.

Upon returning to the apartment, we discovered, with no little exasperation, that A.J. had not been home all evening. When he did arrive drunk, he scared hell out of us with cryptic rantings about Druid gods and rituals, recreating one wherein he had Orrie lie fully clothed on the bed as he placed crossed swords on her breast and chanted incantations, none of which he remembered the next day.

In the Bay we took great risks with our trysts. We would rendezvous in each other's room when Katherine was not in the house, or in the hallway in the dead of night. We would sneak back into the school after it was closed and christen the library tables and classroom desks with the sweat of our loins. And we would pretend to go to the movies and slip away to the beach at night amid the gigantic broken concrete rubble that still littered some places three years after the 1947 hurricane.

There, where most people were afraid to go as it was presumed a refuge for snakes, we would hide amid the giant slabs of concrete and asphalt, seeking out those with an almost horizontal platform or a comfortable place to lean against.

There, beneath the stars and the moon, while the water sang a hypnotic lullaby and the breeze mingled the scent of azaleas and the smell of brine, we would try to escape into each other's body, and try to plan what the future would hold for us.

Orrie wanted marriage, but she had never planned to fall in love with a teen age boy totally unprepared to commit to an all-American middle to upper middle class life. I wanted to escape the confinement of a small town, but I had not expected to escape to the confinement of church and children and community endeavors. We were intellectually compatible when discussing or speculating on art or literature or philosophy, but we were somewhat socially incompatible in agreeing on careers or church or child raising, and particularly the timetable for such things.

By the time I graduated, we had agreed to a summer hiatus on the subject, she finishing some classes at the University of Alabama in Tuscaloosa, and I visiting my father in Canada, the two of us meeting again in Tuscaloosa at the end of the summer.

The three months I spent with Erle did nothing to endear me to him, and confirmed all I had heard about him previously. He still had several acres of greenhouse outside Hamilton, Ontario, and supplied the florists in Hamilton and Toronto with 'tropical plants,' mostly dish gardens potted with miniature cacti and succulents. I worked in the greenhouse, drove the van to deliver to the florists, and earned enough money to buy a used car by the end of the summer, But, at seventeen, I was still a minor and Erle would not sign the export papers so I could leave with my car. He thought he could coerce me to stay and work for him, having visions of me supporting him in his old age. I left him at the end of the summer, free of any desire to ever have anything to do with him again, and joined Orrie in Tuscaloosa.

Orrie and I decided to get married after she commenced her new teaching assignment in Selma, Alabama, and after I found employment there. I tried for months to get a foothold in Selma, working in a gas station and saving the glass dinner ware premiums they gave away, selling Wearever Cookware on commissions that barely paid for the samples we would use to set up housekeeping, and finally returning to New Orleans for several months where I worked as a teletype-PBX operator in a canning factory. I visited Orrie in Selma frequently, seeking job interviews on every trip, and eventually was hired by the local Sears store as a display manager.

In May of 1950 I left Bay St. Louis and never returned as a permanent resident. On January 27th of 1951, I married Orrie two days after my 18th birthday. Katherine had given her permission, but I had failed to get the blood tests in time. On the outskirts of New Orleans we found a JP who overlooked the required tests and performed the ceremony for an exorbitant fee and with uncalled for remarks about our no longer needing to "sneak around in cheap motels."

Foregoing any real honeymoon, we drove to Selma with a brief one night stay over in a small motel hidden amid pine trees. I had bought her a small 1/3 caret diamond engagement ring and simple wedding band, and I promised her someday I'd buy her a large diamond and take her on a real honeymoon.

Our courtship had been fraught with a guilt ridden environment, and our eventual marriage ritual was far from storybook romance. But neither of us nor our marriage suffered from those shortcomings. Our body, mind, and spirit, our sexuality, intellect, and love, gave us a strong bond which I believe is essential to base marriage on. If our marriage failed, it would not be because of what we failed to bring to it initially, for we had communicated honestly and openly with each other, and we were truly in love.

There were many things lacking in my childhood, many opportunities unfulfilled. No one can ever predict what might have been had things been different. But the longer I live, the more I am convinced that my life has been filled with great good fortune. I would not trade those good things to erase what was lacking or fulfill lost opportunities. My only regret is that I can never adequately thank all those who contributed to my learning and to the experience of my life. I have never regretted my marriage, and I never regretted having been raised among the genteel poor.

EPILOGUE

Katherine was born in 1900 and died in 1967 at Keesler Air Force Base Hospital from the after-effects of colon cancer. The last 15 years of her life she maintained

A.J. in her home and enjoyed a career as Librarian in Bay St. Louis where she integrated the library and was instrumental in having the internationally famous black sculptor, Richmond Barthe, honored as the town's most famous citizen during its Centennial Celebration.

Katherine's sister, Thelma Morris, never succeeded in developing the Hamburg property, never remarried, and never suffered the re-appearance of Bob Morris. She continued working at the brokerage the rest of her life, enjoying her courtyard patio apartment on Royal Street in the heart of New Orleans French Quarter, and dying in 1964 of a heart attack in that apartment with Katherine beside her, nursing her during her last days of illness.

A.J. had several long term relationships with older women, most of them alcoholics, but he never married and never had children. He remained a non-offensive soft-core alcoholic and, after Katherine's death, became a hermit living in a small home made cabin in the woods North of the Bay not far from his sister, Thelma. He died at the age of 80 from throat cancer three months before Hurricane Katrina devastated the Gulf Coast..

My sister, Thelma, visited Katherine in Bay St. Louis once at the age of fifteen, and again at the age of seventeen when she left Canada forever. She moved to Florida, had an early career as a magazine cover model, owned her own beauty salons in the Bahamas, and met and was courted by numerous celebrities and world famous politicians while working in the hotel industry in the West Indies. She was married three times, but never had children. She assumed the role of caretaking A.J. after her mother died. She and her third husband operated a nursery for flowering plants back in the woods 25 miles north of Bay St. Louis. Her husband died a month after A.J. did, two months before Hurricane Katrina hit. Thelma survived together with one priceless artifact from her home, a head of her youthful beauty sculpted by Richmond Barthe.

Erle became a full fledged alcoholic in mid-life, the period during which Thelma went to live with her father, then rehabilitated himself before reaching his senior years. Erle married his common law wife, Norah, and outlived both Katherine and Norah before dying in his 90's, as did his father, Ezra, who lived to be 96.

Orrie and I remained married four and a half years and divorced without children, remaining compatible in most respects and differing sharply on the schedule and modis operandi of raising children. At her request, I never intruded upon her life thereafter and lost track of her.

I presumed I would eventually remarry, but never did so into my 70's. The fact that the descendants of 'Mimi' Belzorah Stanselle narrowed down to zero has haunted me, prompted me to write autobiographical works, and produce a documentary film about my family. I am concerned that families with gifted, sensitive, thoughtful people who might make such wonderful parents as Katherine was, seem disillusioned with society and abdicate their participation and genealogical contributions to it.

Fifty-five years after graduating from Bay High School and less than a month before Hurricane Katrina struck Bay St. Louis, I attended a high school class reunion there. It was interesting to note that most of my classmates had exceeded life expectancy for my generation, fewer had succumbed to drugs or alcohol or cancer than succeeding generations fell prey to, and all had enjoyed varying degrees of prosperity into an age where poverty and homelessness still prevail.

Odelle's golden mane and svelte figure had evolved into baldness and a belt line half again that of his youth, but, in addition to a successful career as a Territory Manager in pharmaceutical sales and generations of children, he was still married to his high school sweetheart and he was still leader of the pack emceeing the festivities.

Martin still had most of his hair, generations of children, and wonderful stories of his early career in the Marines and his later career in education. And while some of the ladies could no longer fit into their high school cheerleading and majorette costumes, their faces and personalities were readily identifiable and evocative of wonderful bygone memories.

And yet, for some, social and political issues had not kept pace with the rest of the world. Good people one and all, but some more enlightened than others.

The balance of my life is chronicled in my other autobiographical works, the first published being *Lenny Bruce: The Making Of A Prophet,* a memoir about my ten year collaboration with that controversial nightclub comedian of the 1960's. Other fiction manuscripts are laid in the 1950's and 1960's and are based on my careers and experiences as a cocktail pianist in New Orleans French Quarter, a tour of combat duty in Korea, being a publicist working in Hollywood and the black community of Los Angeles during the civil rights era, a collection of Hollywood short stories, and a science fiction trilogy.

It is my wish that you and I and all on this spaceship earth might "live long and prosper," and perhaps we will fulfill, if not survive, this experience called 'life,' and I shall write even more works. Until you read my works again, I thank you for sharing this part of my life.

THE END

Mrs. A. B. Dubisson
Commercial

Mr. A. B. Dubuisson
Mathematics,
Driving, Mechanics

Mrs. George Curet
English

Mrs. Carl Smith
Music Teacher

Orrie
Librarian

Mrs. N. B. Hall
English
Spanish

(Upper right): The newlyweds.

(Lower center): Lo poses before the statue of Diana in Audubon Park.

(Lower left): Thelma Schmidt poses before Diana. Both pictures shot in the mid 1930's before the shrubbery maze grew up around the life-size bronze statue.

OTHER BOOKS BY WILLIAM KARL THOMAS

All books available from Media Maestro - Book Division, P.O. Box 50672, Tucson, AZ 85703, or online at www.mediamaestro.net/books.htm, Amazon.com, and other online book vendors, or order through your local bookstore via books ISBN number. Website includes descriptions, excerpts, and order forms.

THE GENTEEL POOR

The book you have just read is available in hardcover or an E-edition for your Kindle, Nook, I-pad, or other E-reader, or read it on your computer by downloading Amazon's free E-reader application. Tell your friends they can get the E-edition instantly online for less than the postage it would cost to mail your print copy across the nation.
ISBN #978-1-59663-565-4 . Hardcover: $29.95
ISBN 978-1-62768-000-4 Softcover $9.95
ISBN #978-0-9799477-9-7 Digital edition: $4.99

LENNY BRUCE: THE MAKING OF A PROPHET

William Karl Thomas' intimate and poignant memoir of his ten year collaboration with the most controversial comedian of the 20th century, a martyr to First Amendment rights. The book begins before Bruce's rise to international fame and continues through the night Bruce died.
ISBN #978-0-9799477-0-4 Hardcover: $24.95
ISBN #978-1-62768-003-5 Softcover $9.95
ISBN #978-0-9799477-4-2 Digital E-edition $4.99

CLEO
A novel about a beautiful and talented black female journalist who is an intimate friend of black entertainment and political celebrities during the turbulent civil rights era in the 1950's and 1960's. Her professional and private life takes a quantum leap when she crosses paths with a cynical but equally talented white male publicist.
ISBN #978-1-62768-002-8 Softcover $9.95
ISBN #978-0-9799477-6-6 Digital E-edition $4.99

THE JOSAN AND THE JEE
A novel about three women who survived massacres and rape during The Korean War, and their intimate relationship with an American GI dealing with his own demons from his failed marriage to his unfaithful stateside wife to his contentious relationship with his military boss.
ISBN #978-1-62768-001-1 Softcover $9.95
ISBN #978-0-9799477-5-9 Digital E-edition $4.99

THE PIANO MAN
In New Orleans French Quarter during the 1950's, a young male cocktail pianist's life is complicated by four beautiful women; two young women from opposite poles of society who love him in their diverse ways, and two middle aged women who seek to control him for their own secret reasons.
ISBN #978-1-62768-005-9 Softcover $14.95
ISBN #978-1-62768-006-6 Digital Edition $4.99

MORE BOOKS ON THE NEXT PAGE

HOLLYWOOD TALES FROM THE OUTER FRINGE

Thomas' career brought him in contact with 'A' list celebrities and the armies of 'little people' who served them. This anthology of 12 short stories reveals the intimate relationship between the two set against a historically accurate 1950's-1960's background..
ISBN #978-0-9799477-3-5 Softcover $9.95
ISBN #978-0-9799477-7-3 Digital E-edition $4.99

A PLACE FOR US

Wendy Wolf entered an iron lung at the age of four and emerged a polio survivor whose life illustrates the challenges of opportunity and acceptance people with disabilities face and the triumphs and successes this extraordinary woman achieved.
ISBN #978-0-9799477-2-8 Hardcover $29.95
ISBN #978-1-62768-004-2 Softcover $9.95
ISBN #978-0-9799477-8-0 Digital edition: $4.99

SOON TO BE RELEASED BOOKS BY WILLIAM KARL THOMAS

IMMORTAL: A SCIENCE FICTION TRILOGY

A millennium into the future, three alien archeologists attempt to determine how humanity self destructed themselves and their planet. Their discovery of a dormant android guarding a human gene bank on a Saturnian moon leads to a conflict among them regarding humanity's potential future. Share the alien's discovery of human evolution and the turning points of earth's civilizations.
ISBN #978-1-62768-007-3 Softcover $14.95
ISBN #978-1-62768-008-0 Digital E-edition $4.99

www.ingramcontent.com/pod-product-compliance
Lightning Source LLC
Chambersburg PA
CBHW060821050426
42453CB00008B/527